THE VIETNAM WAR

Reg Grant

WORLD ALMANAC® LIBRARY

Please visit our web site at: www.worldalmanaclibrary.com
For a free color catalog describing World Almanac® Library's list of high-quality books
and multimedia programs, call 1-800-848-2928 (USA) or 1-800-387-3178 (Canada).
World Almanac® Library's fax: (414) 332-3567.

Library of Congress Cataloging-in-Publication Data

Grant, Reg G.
    The Vietnam War / by Reg Grant.
        p. cm. — (Atlas of conflicts)
    Includes bibliographical references and index.
    Contents: The first Indochina war — More U.S. involvement — Search and destroy: 1965-1967 —
A turning point: 1968 — Vietnamization: 1969-1971 — Easter offensive to Christmas bombing —
Communism triumphs — Aftermath.
    ISBN 0-8368-5667-8 (lib. bdg.)
    ISBN 0-8368-5674-0 (softcover)
    1. Vietnamese Conflict, 1961-1975—Juvenile literature. [1. Vietnamese Conflict, 1961-1975—
Maps for children.] I. Title. II. Series.
  DS557.7.G7   2004
  959.704'3—dc22   2004045160

This North American edition first published in 2005 by
World Almanac® Library
330 West Olive Street, Suite 100
Milwaukee, WI 53212 USA

Produced by Arcturus Publishing Limited.
Series concept: Alex Woolf
Editor: Philip de Ste. Croix
Designer: Simon Burrough
Cartography: The Map Studio
Consultant: Paul Cornish, Imperial War Museum, London
Picture researcher: Thomas Mitchell

World Almanac® Library editor: Jim Mezzanotte
World Almanac® Library design: Steve Schraenkler
World Almanac® Library production: Jessica Morris

All the photographs in this book, with the exception of those listed below, were supplied by
Getty Images and are reproduced here with their permission.
Camera Press: pages 41, 50.
Popperfoto: pages 46, 47.

Printed in Italy

1 2 3 4 5 6 7 8 9 08 07 06 05 04

CONTENTS

CHAPTER 1
THE FIRST INDOCHINA WAR

Japanese troops move into Vietnam in July 1941, beginning their four-year occupation of the country. At the time, Vietnam was part of French Indochina, a French colony.

Vietnam is a communist country in southeast Asia with a population of about 80 million. Its recorded history stretches back more than 2,000 years. In the second half of the nineteenth century, at a time when European countries were extending their rule over much of Asia and Africa, the French made Vietnam part of French Indochina. This French colony also included Vietnam's neighbors, Cambodia and Laos.

From the start, Vietnamese nationalists opposed French rule, but the French colonial authorities harshly repressed all opposition. In the early decades of the twentieth century, many nationalists took refuge abroad. One such nationalist was Ho Chi Minh, the son of a Vietnamese official. In 1920, while living in France, Ho became a communist. From then on, he dedicated his life to two goals: achieving national independence for Vietnam and establishing a communist society in which private ownership of industry and land would be abolished.

The French remained firmly in control of Indochina until World War II (1939–45). Early in the war, Germany invaded and occupied France. As a result, France was in no position to aid its colonists in Indochina when they came under pressure from Japan, an ally of Germany in the war and a rising power in Asia. In 1941, the French colonial authorities were forced to allow Japanese troops to occupy Indochina. Although the Japanese left the French officially in control, they effectively ruled the colony.

In the same year, Ho Chi Minh and other Vietnamese nationalists founded a guerrilla organization to fight both the Japanese and the French. They called it the *Vietnam Doc Lap Dong Minh Hoi* ("League for the Independence of Vietnam"),

NATIONALIST OR COMMUNIST?

Tran Ngoc Danh, a colleague of Viet Minh leader Ho Chi Minh, wrote:
"How many times in my life have I been asked: you who know Ho Chi Minh so well, can you say whether he is a nationalist or a communist? The answer is simple: Ho Chi Minh is both. For him, nationalism and communism, the end and the means, complement one another . . ."
—Quoted in *Historical Atlas of the Vietnam War,* Summers and Karnow

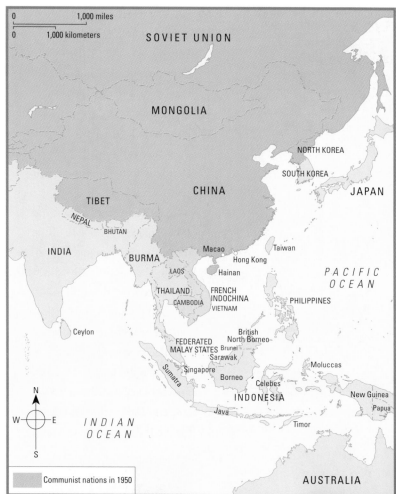

In the early 1950s, French Indochina bordered an area of Asia that was largely under communist rule. The United States considered Indochina to be in the front line of its fight against the spread of communism.

control of large areas of northern Vietnam. In March 1945, the Japanese abolished French rule in Indochina, but the following August Japan surrendered to the United States and its allies. This surrender left a power vacuum in Vietnam that the Viet Minh were quick to exploit. On September 2, 1945, in the northern city of Hanoi, Ho declared Vietnam independent under a Viet Minh government. In the southern city of Saigon, however, which was occupied by British troops, the French regained control.

At first, the two sides reached a compromise. In March 1946, the Viet Minh and the French agreed that Vietnam would be a "Free State" within the French empire. But the following November,

or Viet Minh for short. The leaders of the Viet Minh, including Ho and the organization's chief military commander, Vo Nguyen Giap, were communists. As the name of the guerrillas suggests, however, they appealed above all to the Vietnamese desire for national independence.

During World War II, the Viet Minh received support from the United States, which had been at war with Japan since December of 1941. Ho's guerrillas fought the Japanese with increasing success and won

General Vo Nguyen Giap commanded the Viet Minh forces during the First Indochina War. This picture of Giap is from 1966, when he was North Vietnam's Minister of Defense.

Viet Minh guerrillas cross an improvised bridge during their struggle against the French in 1953. Traveling almost entirely on foot in Vietnam's rough terrain, the Viet Minh were formidable fighters.

fighting broke out between the French and the Viet Minh, first in the northern port city of Haiphong and then in Hanoi. The Viet Minh army withdrew from these cities to the countryside, where they launched a guerrilla war against the French.

A NEW FIGHT
Until 1949, it seemed the French would be able to contain the guerrillas. In that year, however, communists led by Mao Zedong took control of Vietnam's huge neighbor to the north, China. Supplied with arms and equipment by the Chinese communists, the Viet Minh were able to take the initiative. Much of Vietnam is mountainous and covered in thick jungle. It was

an ideal place for the guerrillas, who could hide from view and then ambush the more heavily armed French troops. In 1951, the Viet Minh launched a major offensive. Although the French were able to defend the densely populated area of the Red River Delta in the north, the Viet Minh took control of many French outposts in rural areas.

France lacked the resources to sustain a war in Indochina over a long period, and it soon became dependent on U.S. support. In general, the United States favored independence for countries under European colonial rule. By 1947, however, the Cold War had begun. In this struggle for dominance between the United States and

"ENDURING MEN . . ."

Major Marcel Bigeard, a French paratrooper in Vietnam, expressed his admiration for the Viet Minh guerrillas: *"I can tell you they became the greatest infantry in the world: these enduring men capable of covering 50 kilometres in the night on the strength of a bowl of rice, with running shoes, and then singing their way into battle . . ."*

—Quoted in *Vietnam: The Ten Thousand Day War*, Michael Maclear

the communist Soviet Union, the United States sought to stop the spread of communism, which it considered to be a global threat. After the communist takeover of China in 1949, the United States became worried about further communist expansion in Asia. When communist North Korea invaded South Korea in 1950, U.S. and United Nations (UN) troops were sent in to resist the invasion. At the same time, the United States also provided money and arms to the French to fight the Viet Minh.

By the end of 1953, France's position in Vietnam was becoming desperate. The military strength of the Viet Minh had grown, and they had also gained widespread support among a people eager to be free of colonial rule. The French had set up a government under a traditional Vietnamese ruler, Emperor Bao Dai, but it attracted little support.

Seeking to regain the initiative, French commanders decided to establish a powerful base at Dien

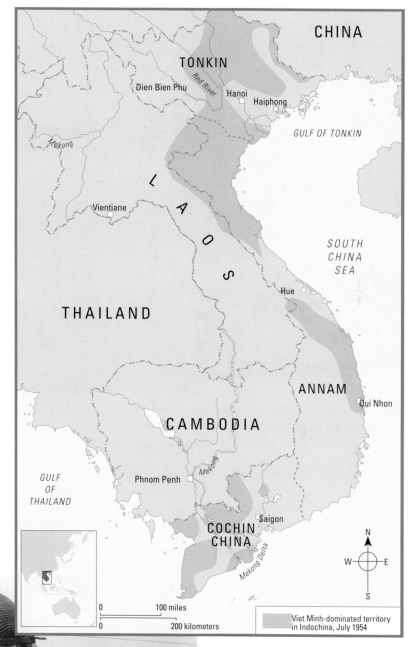

Under French rule, Vietnam was divided into three parts: Tonkin, Annam, and Cochin China. In 1954, the Viet Minh dominated most of Tonkin outside the major cities, as well as part of Annam and much of Cochin China.

A French doctor treats a Vietnamese soldier during the siege of Dien Bien Phu in 1954. Thousands of anticommunist Vietnamese fought alongside the French against the Viet Minh.

7

French paratroopers float to the ground in Dien Bien Phu. The base was shelled by Viet Minh artillery positioned in the surrounding mountains.

Bien Phu, a remote site in northern Vietnam close to the border with Laos. The commanders hoped the base would help block the Viet Minh supply lines bringing men and arms into Vietnam and prevent an expected Viet Minh attack on Laos. Seeing an opportunity to inflict a decisive defeat on the French, the Viet Minh assembled powerful infantry forces around Dien Bien Phu and hauled artillery up mountainsides around the French base. In March 1954, the guerrillas launched their attack. The French garrison, which consisted chiefly of elite parachute battalions, resisted fiercely. But they were surrounded and outnumbered, and they could only receive supplies by air.

France's only hope of avoiding a humiliating defeat was to appeal to the United States. French and U.S. military commanders devised a plan for a massive aerial bombardment by U.S. aircraft to destroy the Viet Minh forces besieging the base at Dien Bien Phu. U.S. president Dwight D. Eisenhower, however, rejected the idea of involving U.S. forces directly in support of the French.

Vietnamese communist leader Ho Chi Minh was known as "Uncle Ho," but he was ruthless in his pursuit of a united, communist Vietnam.

DEFEAT AT DIEN BIEN PHU On May 8, 1954, the Viet Minh finally overran the French forces at Dien Bien Phu. On the same day, a peace conference opened in Geneva, Switzerland, to discuss an end to the war. The following July, a peace agreement called the Geneva Accords granted Vietnam, Laos, and Cambodia independence from France. But Vietnam

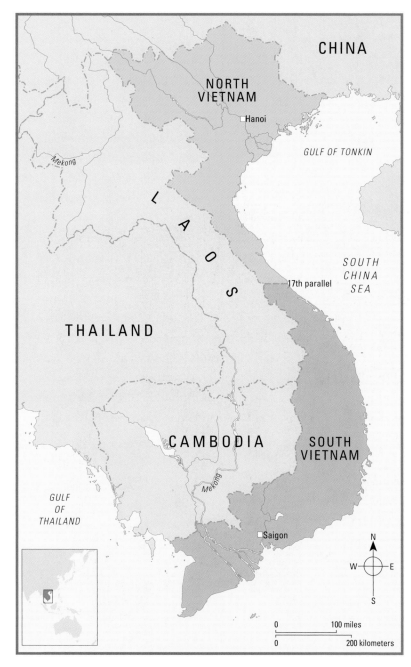

The Democratic Republic of Vietnam (North Vietnam) was separated from the Republic of Vietnam (South Vietnam) by a demilitarized zone (DMZ) along the 17th parallel.

General Henri Navarre, the French commander in Indochina at the time of the defeat at Dien Bien Phu, criticized U.S. president Eisenhower's decision not to provide air support: *"There is no doubt that if the American air force had been heavily involved . . . Dien Bien Phu would certainly have been saved. The US would not have had to become involved later as it was obliged to do."*
—Quoted in *Vietnam: The Ten Thousand Day War*, Michael Maclear

was divided in two, with Ho and the Viet Minh taking control north of the 17th parallel and Emperor Bao Dai ruling south of the parallel.

According to the Geneva Accords, this division would be temporary. Vietnam was to be reunited in two years' time, after democratic elections were held to choose a government for the whole country. No such elections, however, were ever held. In the north, Ho established the Democratic Republic of Vietnam, which was usually called North Vietnam. Ruled by the communist Vietnamese Workers' Party, North Vietnam became a communist state like the Soviet Union, China, North Korea, and various countries in Eastern Europe. In the south, the Republic of Vietnam was established. Known as South Vietnam, it was first ruled by Emperor Bao Dai. He was soon replaced by Ngo Dinh Diem, a tough leader who had the backing of the United States.

After the Geneva Accords, about 900,000 Vietnamese, believing there was no place for them in a communist state, chose to move from North Vietnam to South Vietnam. At the same time, some 100,000 Viet Minh fighters withdrew from South Vietnam and went north. The division of Vietnam was destined to last for more than 20 years.

CHAPTER 2
MORE U.S. INVOLVEMENT

By 1962, U.S. Army officers were "advising" South Vietnamese soldiers who were fighting communist-led guerrillas, and U.S. helicopter pilots were flying them into battle.

The United States regarded the French defeat in Indochina and the establishment of a communist state in North Vietnam as a serious setback in its efforts to resist the worldwide spread of communism. U.S. officials were determined to prevent any further expansion of communist rule in Southeast Asia. To this end, from 1954 onward they sought to support South Vietnam, with the goal of turning it into a stable country that could defend itself against an attack from North Vietnam—or against subversion by guerrillas working within its borders. In 1956, the United States established the Military Assistance Advisory Group in South Vietnam's capital, Saigon. The group later became the Military Assistance Command, Vietnam, or MACV. The United States provided money, arms, and military advisers to help strengthen the Army of the Republic of South Vietnam, or ARVN.

U.S. officials understood that the future of South Vietnam depended as much on good government as on a strong military. Ngo Dinh Diem, however, soon proved to be a poor leader. Diem's repressive regime

South Vietnamese president Ngo Dinh Diem visits New York in May 1957. At the time, he enjoyed the full support of the United States, but U.S. officials later considered him to be a liability.

closed down opposition newspapers, and the secret police, the Can Lao, inspired fear among the people. In addition, Diem was a Catholic in a mostly Buddhist country, and he aroused the hostility of Vietnamese Buddhists. Diem failed to carry through land reform in rural areas that might have won peasants over to his side. Instead, he raised taxes and replaced locally elected village leaders with his own appointed officials. Soon discontent was rife in the countryside. In 1957 and 1958, isolated terrorist attacks occurred, including the assassination of government officials.

In May 1959, the North Vietnamese government decided that the time was ripe for promoting guerrilla war in South Vietnam, with the aim of overthrowing Diem and reuniting Vietnam under communist rule. Thousands of experienced Viet Minh cadres (officers) in North Vietnam were sent back into South Vietnam with orders to begin building up a guerrilla movement in the countryside. Work began on organizing a supply route from the North to the South through Laos and Cambodia—a complex pattern of roads and paths that became known as the Ho Chi Minh Trail. Arms and men were also carried into the South by sea, mainly by small boats sailing down to the Mekong Delta south of Saigon.

The guerrilla movement in South Vietnam called itself the National Liberation Front, or NLF,

Supplies from North Vietnam were carried to guerrillas in the South on jungle trails in Laos and Cambodia and by small boats along the coast. Many of the supplies originated in China.

DOMINO THEORY

A major justification for U.S. support for South Vietnam was the "domino theory"—the belief that if South Vietnam fell to communism, many other countries in Asia would also fall, like a row of dominoes. As a U.S. senator, John F. Kennedy stated in 1956: *"Burma, Thailand, India, Japan, the Philippines and obviously Laos and Cambodia are among those whose security would be threatened if the red tide of communism overflowed into Vietnam."*

—Quoted in *America in Vietnam*, Guenter Lewy

although to the United States the guerrillas were always the Viet Cong, or VC. Founded in 1960, the NLF was careful to appeal to Vietnamese nationalism, describing the guerrilla war as a continuation of the struggle previously fought against the French, with the United States now the "imperialist" power.

The NLF swiftly built up a strong position in rural South Vietnam. Young men left their villages—sometimes voluntarily, sometimes not—and traveled to remote areas for training as full-time members of the guerrilla army. They made up the Viet Cong "main force," capable of taking on the ARVN and, later, U.S. forces. At the same time, many peasants who stayed in the villages constituted "part-time" aid to the guerrillas. They not only provided intelligence and food supplies but also planted

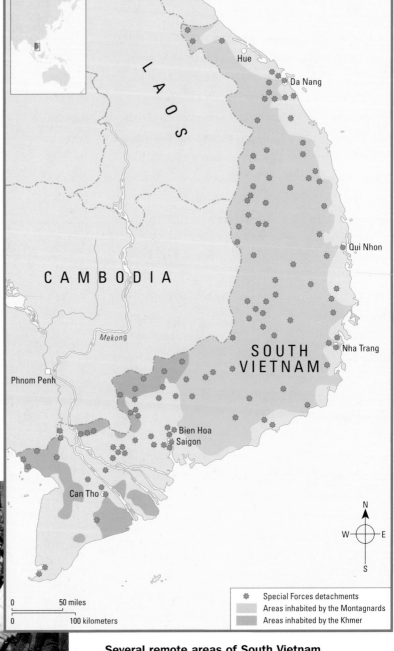

A U.S. military adviser (second from left) looks on as an ARVN officer examines captured papers.

Several remote areas of South Vietnam were inhabited by people who were not ethnic Vietnamese. U.S. Special Forces were able to organize many of them for anticommunist activity.

U.S. TROOPS IN SOUTH VIETNAM
The U.S. military commitment to South Vietnam rose steeply between 1960 and 1964.

	1960	1961	1962	1963	1964
U.S. military personnel	875	3,164	11,326	16,263	23,310
U.S. deaths in action	0	1	31	77	137

booby-trap bombs or took part in ambushes of military patrols.

The first U.S. casualties in Vietnam were military advisers wounded in a Viet Cong raid at Bien Hoa in July 1959. The following January, guerrillas defeated an ARVN force northeast of Saigon. The United States responded by increasing its force of military advisers in South Vietnam, from about 1,000 in 1960 to more than 11,000 by the end of 1962, including 300 helicopter pilots who went into battle alongside the ARVN.

COUNTERINSURGENCY Strategies for counterinsurgency—the name given to tactics designed to defeat guerrilla operations—were a hot topic at this time. A new U.S. president, John F. Kennedy, believed that actions against communist-led "national liberation movements" were going to be a crucial part of the ongoing cold war. Kennedy was an advocate of the Green Berets, U.S. Special Forces troops who were trained in unconventional warfare techniques. Beginning in 1962, the Green Berets were sent in to organize resistance to the Viet Cong among the Montagnard tribespeople—non-Vietnamese who lived in remote, mountainous areas of Vietnam. The Montagnard Civilian Irregular Defense Groups, or CIDGs, were led and armed by the Green Berets. They had some success within Viet Cong-dominated areas, but their effect on the war was marginal.

Another form of counterinsurgency was the Strategic Hamlets program, which the United States also initiated in 1962. This program involved moving South Vietnamese peasants out of their villages and into large fortified settlements, where they could be defended from the guerrillas and, in theory, won over to the government's side. In practice, however, nothing was done to win the "hearts and minds" of the rural population. The Strategic Hamlets were little better than concentration camps, and being herded into them only made the peasants more hostile to the South Vietnamese government.

At this time, U.S. planes also began spraying chemical defoliants from the air. These chemicals were meant to destroy crops being grown to feed the Viet Cong and to clear areas of vegetation that might

U.S. planes, loaded with chemical defoliants, fly on a mission to spray an area of South Vietnam where guerrillas are active.

A Buddhist monk burns himself to death in South Vietnam to protest the policies of President Diem. The majority of South Vietnamese were Buddhists, but Diem was a Catholic.

GULF OF TONKIN RESOLUTION

The resolution that the U.S. Congress passed on August 7, 1964, after the Gulf of Tonkin incident, denounced the alleged attacks on U.S. warships as "*part of a deliberate and systematic campaign of aggression that the Communist regime in North Vietnam has been waging . . .*" and declared "*. . . that the Congress approve and support the determination of the President, as Commander in Chief, to take all necessary measures to repel any armed attack against the forces of the United States and to prevent further aggression.*"

be used by the guerrillas as cover. Defoliant spraying would eventually expand into a large-scale—and highly controversial—operation, but it had little immediate effect in restricting guerrilla activity.

By 1963, the Viet Cong were in effective control of a large and expanding area of the South Vietnamese countryside. At the same time, Diem's position as the country's leader was collapsing. His rule had grown increasingly dictatorial and incompetent. Vietnamese Buddhists were in open conflict with the Diem regime, and the American public was shocked by images of Buddhist monks burning themselves to death in the streets as a protest against Diem's rule.

In the fall of 1963, the U.S. government secretly gave its approval to a military coup by a group of South Vietnamese generals, led by General Duong Van Minh. On November 1, Diem was arrested and then killed, along with his brother Nhu. Within three weeks of Diem's death, John F. Kennedy was assassinated in Dallas, Texas, and Vice president Lyndon B. Johnson became U.S. president. Johnson continued the U.S. policy of supporting South Vietnam against what the United States called "communist aggression."

General Minh and his colleagues, however, proved even less capable than Diem of creating a stable government that could defeat the guerrillas. They soon squabbled bitterly among themselves and coup followed coup. In March 1964,

President Johnson (seated) calls on the U.S. Congress to support military action in Vietnam after the Gulf of Tonkin incident.

Below: The report of a second attack on the USS *Maddox* led to retaliatory air strikes by U.S. planes.

U.S. secretary of defense Robert McNamara visited Saigon to assess the situation. He concluded that South Vietnam was on the verge of total collapse. The United States either had to admit defeat and allow the country to fall to the communists or increase its own military involvement in the war.

The number of U.S. military advisers in South Vietnam was consequently increased to 23,000, and General William C. Westmoreland was sent to head the MACV. But McNamara believed that any actions against the guerrillas in the South would simply buy some time. The only way to save South Vietnam would be to force the North Vietnamese government to call a halt to the fighting.

GULF OF TONKIN The United States believed an invasion of North Vietnam was out of the question, because it would have led the Chinese to send in troops—as they had when U.S.-UN forces invaded North Korea in 1950. U.S. covert operations, however, had been taking place in North Vietnam and Laos since 1961. In January 1964 President Johnson secretly authorized "hit-and-run raids" by gunboats along the coast of North Vietnam.

U.S. warships sometimes patrolled the Gulf of Tonkin to gather intelligence in support of these secret raids. On August 2, 1964, one such warship, a destroyer called the USS *Maddox,* was sailing about 10 miles (16 kilometers) off the coast of North Vietnam when it was attacked by North Vietnamese torpedo boats. The USS *Maddox* drove off the boats with the help of aircraft from the carrier USS *Ticonderoga.* After this attack, President Johnson announced that any further "unprovoked military action" by North Vietnam would lead to "grave consequences."

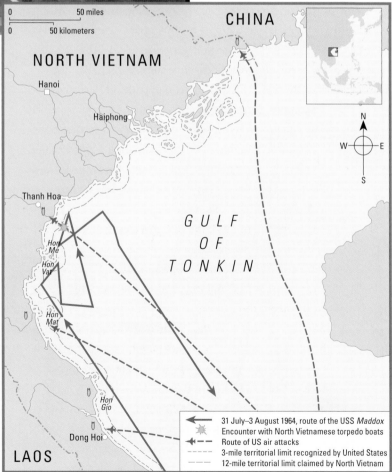

CHINA

NORTH VIETNAM

Hanoi

Haiphong

Thanh Hoa

Hon Me

Hon Vat

Hon Mat

GULF OF TONKIN

Hon Gio

Dong Hoi

LAOS

0   50 miles
0   50 kilometers

N
W — E
S

→ 31 July–3 August 1964, route of the USS *Maddox*
✸ Encounter with North Vietnamese torpedo boats
◄— Route of US air attacks
----- 3-mile territorial limit recognized by United States
— — 12-mile territorial limit claimed by North Vietnam

Two days later, on the night of August 4, the USS *Maddox* and another destroyer reported that they had once again been attacked by enemy vessels. There has been controversy over whether this attack did occur, but nonetheless it had far-reaching consequences. President Johnson ordered immediate air strikes in retaliation, and U.S. aircraft bombed ports in North Vietnam. More importantly, on August 7 the U.S. Congress passed what became known as the Gulf of Tonkin Resolution. This resolution allowed Johnson to escalate U.S. military involvement in Vietnam without a formal declaration of war by Congress.

ROLLING THUNDER

The next U.S. bombing raids on North Vietnam followed in February 1965, in retaliation for guerrilla attacks on U.S. bases in South Vietnam. Then, on March 2, 1965, the United States initiated a sustained bombing campaign against North Vietnam called "Rolling Thunder." Although it had a number of interruptions, this campaign continued until October 1968.

ROLLING THUNDER STATISTICS

The 1965–1968 Rolling Thunder bombing campaign against North Vietnam was carried out on a massive scale:

Sorties flown by U.S. Navy and Air Force fighter bombers	304,000
Sorties flown by B-52 bombers over North Vietnam	2,380
Bombs dropped (in tons)	592,000
U.S. aircraft lost in combat	922

The purpose of Rolling Thunder was to persuade North Vietnam to call off the fight in South Vietnam. The United States varied the intensity of the bombing raids, periodically stepping up or reducing the attacks as a way of bullying or coaxing the North Vietnamese into stopping the war. Many targets were permanently off-limits—mostly to avoid provoking North Vietnam's powerful supporters, China and the Soviet Union. Although the rules of engagement changed from time

North Vietnamese women operate a Soviet-supplied antiaircraft gun. North Vietnam's effective air defenses took a heavy toll on U.S. aircraft.

A low-flying U.S. fighter plane casts a shadow near a bomb-shattered bridge in North Vietnam during the Rolling Thunder bombing campaign.

to time, for much of the period no attacks were made on Haiphong port, the main entry point for Soviet supplies to North Vietnam.

The bombing cost the United States heavy losses. The North Vietnamese had Soviet-supplied antiaircraft guns and missiles, as well as Soviet MiG fighter planes. U.S. pilots were forced to observe many limits that restricted them in combat. At first, for example, they were not allowed to attack missile sites, because to do so would have risked widening the war by injuring or killing Soviet technicians who assisted the North Vietnamese.

Today, the Rolling Thunder campaign is generally recognized to have been a failure. It inflicted a great deal of damage on North Vietnam's industries, military installations, and transport systems, and it is also believed to have killed more than 50,000 civilians. The bombing had no decisive military effect, however, and if anything it stiffened North Vietnamese resistance. It also helped fuel the antiwar protest movements that arose in the United States and other countries in response to the conflict in Vietnam.

The Rolling Thunder bombing campaign was carried out mostly by U.S. fighter jets flying from bases in South Vietnam and from aircraft carriers, with B-52 bombers also taking part. For fear of bringing China into the war, air strikes were not allowed close to the Chinese border.

Chinese buffer zone (prohibited area)
Restricted targeting zone (30 nautical miles)
Restricted targeting zone (10 nautical miles)
US 7th Fleet (Task Force 77)
US airbase (jets)
US airbase (B-52)

CHAPTER 3
SEARCH AND DESTROY: 1965–1967

By 1965, the South Vietnamese government had lost control of most of rural South Vietnam. About 70 percent of South Vietnam's villages were in the hands of the communists. The South Vietnamese army (ARVN) was demoralized and suffered from poor leadership. It was no match for the communist forces, which now contained not only Viet Cong guerrillas but also soldiers from the North Vietnamese Army (NVA) who had come into South Vietnam from the Ho Chi Minh Trail. The communists were firmly in control of territory just 18 miles (30 km) from Saigon.

U.S. Marines come ashore from landing craft on a beach in South Vietnam in August 1965. Although originally deployed to defend U.S. bases, U.S. Marines soon took on an offensive role in Vietnam.

From 1965 to 1967, communist guerrillas dominated large areas of the South Vietnamese countryside. At times, U.S. forces penetrated deep inside these hostile areas in an effort to seek out and destroy the enemy.

B-52 bombers, based in Thailand or on the distant islands of Guam or Okinawa, flew many thousands of missions during the war, hitting targets in Vietnam, Cambodia, and Laos.

The U.S. government had hoped that if the ARVN troops were given arms and training, they would do the fighting—and suffer any casualties. But now it was clear that only a large-scale commitment of U.S. combat troops could prevent a communist victory. On March 8, 1965, the first combat force of U.S. Marines landed in South Vietnam at Da Nang. By the end of the year, more than 180,000 U.S. military personnel were in South Vietnam, supported by an awesome supply operation across the Pacific.

The United States was not the only country to send in troops to defend the South Vietnamese government. Soldiers from Australia, New Zealand, South Korea, Thailand, and the Philippines—all members of the Southeast Asia Treaty Organization (SEATO)—fought alongside U.S. troops. From 1965 to 1969, however, the conflict in Vietnam was almost entirely the United States' war, with these allies and even the ARVN itself playing a relatively small role in the fighting. European allies, including Britain, stayed out of the Vietnam War.

In theory, the struggle between forces from the world's greatest military power and the lightly armed Viet Cong and NVA infantry appeared one-sided. In reality, the U.S. forces, led by General Westmoreland, faced a difficult task. Westmoreland was not allowed to invade North Vietnam, for fear of widening the war, and he was not allowed to use nuclear weapons. The U.S. government also refused him permission to send major forces into Laos or Cambodia to block the communist supply routes down South Vietnam's long land border. B-52 bombers subjected the Ho Chi Minh Trail to massive attacks, but the attacks did not stop the movement of men and supplies. The Viet Cong and NVA were able to replace losses in South Vietnam with fresh arrivals from the North.

With their aircraft, warships, and artillery, U.S. forces deployed a truly amazing quantity and variety of firepower in South Vietnam. In line with traditional U.S. military thinking, Westmoreland believed that the way to win the war was to engage the enemy in combat and use this firepower to destroy its forces. But this

FULL-SCALE COMMITMENT

Between 1965 and 1968, the U.S. military commitment in Vietnam was at its height, both in terms of number of troops and number of soldiers killed:

	1965	1966	1967	1968
U.S. military personnel	184,300	385,300	485,600	536,100
U.S. deaths in action	1,369	5,008	9,378	14,592

Viet Cong guerrillas move along the waterways of the Mekong Delta, south of Saigon, in 1966. Many villages in the delta were guerrilla strongholds.

conflict, unlike a conventional war, had no front line where the enemy would stand and fight. South Vietnam was a country well suited to guerrilla warfare, whether it took place in the mountainous jungle of the Central Highlands, the waterways of the Mekong Delta, or the densely populated rice fields where the guerrillas could hide among the villagers.

Both the Viet Cong and the NVA infantry proved to be elusive enemies, skilled in evading combat until a moment of their own choosing. So Westmoreland developed a strategy of "search and destroy"—first seek out the enemy, then call in the firepower.

AIR MOBILITY In Vietnam, tanks and other vehicles were of limited use, because they could easily be ambushed. For mobility, U.S. ground forces relied primarily on fleets of helicopters. These helicopters could carry troops rapidly to battles, ferry supplies to U.S. firebases deep inside hostile territory, evacuate the wounded, and, in the case of gunships, even provide airborne firepower.

In November 1965, U.S. forces faced their first major test in South Vietnam, at the battle of the

The battle of the Ia Drang Valley began with an NVA attack on a U.S. camp at Plei Me. U.S. troops flew in by helicopter to landing zone X-Ray. After two days of fighting, the NVA withdrew.

Ia Drang Valley. This battle took place in the remote Central Highlands, where a substantial number of NVA troops had arrived from the Ho Chi Minh Trail. U.S. military commanders were concerned that the NVA might push down from the Central Highlands to the sea, effectively cutting South Vietnam in half.

The newly formed U.S. 1st Cavalry Division was based in the area, at An Khe, near Pleiku. With about 400 helicopters, the 1st Cavalry was the U.S. Army's first division created specifically to fight airmobile warfare. A battalion of the 1st Cavalry flew in to relieve a Special Forces base at Plei Me, near the Cambodian border, which had come under NVA attack. The air cavalry and the NVA engaged in a fierce battle. U.S. artillery and aircraft—which included B-52 bombers—subjected the NVA to heavy bombardment. In two days' fighting, NVA troops suffered an estimated 2,000 casualties before disappearing back into the jungle.

The U.S. Army rated the Ia Drang Valley battle a considerable success. It certainly showed that the introduction of U.S. forces could prevent a swift communist victory in South Vietnam. But the battle also revealed what a tough fight U.S. soldier would face. At one helicopter landing zone (LZ), a force of 400 U.S. airborne troops, encircled by the NVA, suffered 279 casualties in a day's fighting.

IRON TRIANGLE At first, the United States mostly fought a defensive campaign while it built up troop strength and logistical support. By the end of 1966, however, with more than 385,000 U.S. soldiers in South Vietnam, General Westmoreland was ready to take the offensive with search and destroy operations on a large scale. The goal of these operations was to seize control of areas in South Vietnam that were currently controlled by the guerrillas, and to inflict heavy losses on the enemy.

One guerrilla-dominated region was the "Iron Triangle," an area only 30 miles (50 km) from Saigon. In this area, the Viet Cong had constructed elaborate tunnel

POLITICAL WARFARE

Criticizing U.S. policy at this stage of the war, Henry Kissinger, who would be U.S. secretary of state from 1969 to 1975, wrote:

"We fought a military war; our opponents fought a political one . . . We lost sight of one of the cardinal [main] maxims of guerrilla war: the guerrilla wins if he does not lose; the conventional army loses if it does not win."

—Quoted in *America in Vietnam*, Guenter Lewy

The U.S. Air Cavalry rides into action during an operation in 1967. Before the Vietnam War, helicopters had never been used in large formations.

systems with concealed entrances, creating underground fortresses from which their forces could launch attacks. The guerrillas also had the support of local villagers, many of whom were part-time members of the Viet Cong.

In January 1967, Operation Cedar Falls was launched in the Iron Triangle. It was meant to be a "hammer and anvil" operation. On the southwestern side of the area, U.S. and ARVN troops took up blocking positions to form the "anvil." Helicopter and ground attacks from the north and west would provide the hammer. Between the hammer and anvil, the Viet Cong would be crushed.

The operation lasted 19 days, and it went much as planned. U.S. and ARVN forces occupied the Triangle. Volunteers known as "tunnel rats" explored the network of tunnels, unearthing large quantities of supplies and stacks of documents that provided details of Viet Cong and NVA military plans. The tunnels were destroyed and areas of forest cleared by bulldozer.

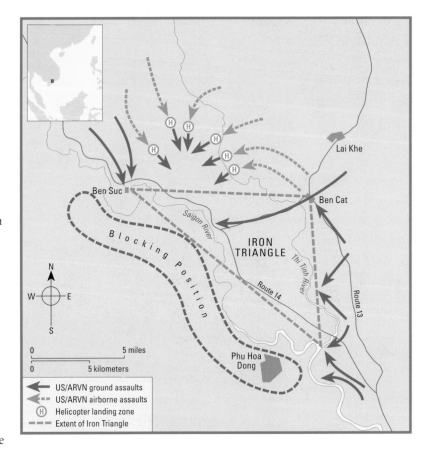

Lai Khe

Ben Suc

Ben Cat

Saigon River

Blocking Position

IRON TRIANGLE

Thi Tinh River

Route 14

Route 13

Phu Hoa Dong

N
W — E
S

| 0 | | 5 miles |
| 0 | | 5 kilometers |

➤ US/ARVN ground assaults
➤ US/ARVN airborne assaults
Ⓗ Helicopter landing zone
— — — Extent of Iron Triangle

Operation Cedar Falls, January 1967.

Soldiers from the U.S. 25th Infantry Division leap from a helicopter near Cu Chi during Operation Cedar Falls.

After searching one of the tunnels dug by Viet Cong guerrillas in the Iron Triangle region near Saigon, a U.S. soldier is given water by one of his comrades. The tunnels were subsequently sealed and blown up.

FREE-FIRE ZONES

Villages in South Vietnam were sometimes cleared of their peasant populations to create "free-fire zones." A U.S. official described this process in 1967:

"The inhabitants are allowed time to pack their belongings and collect their livestock and then are moved to one of the 65 refugee camps in the province. Shortly thereafter the hamlet is destroyed . . . friendly forces continue to receive fire from such hamlets and encounter mines, but they are no longer inhibited from returning fire and calling in artillery and air strikes."

—Quoted in *Guerrilla Warfare*, Robin Corbett

Most of the Viet Cong forces, however, managed to disappear into the jungle, and fighting was relatively light. Only days after Operation Cedar Falls ended, guerrillas were once more operating in the area.

CIVILIAN COSTS One of the first U.S. actions in Operation Cedar Falls was the destruction of the village of Ben Suc, located on the edge of the Iron Triangle. Airborne troops descended on the village, interrogated the population, and arrested suspected Viet Cong members. The villagers were taken to a refugee camp and Ben Suc was burned to the ground. Witnessed by journalists, the village's destruction aroused controversy in the United States, where a vocal antiwar movement was gathering strength.

The fate of Ben Suc was not an isolated event. When U.S. soldiers took on guerrillas in populated rural areas, deploying their massive firepower, the local people inevitably suffered. U.S. forces operated under rules that forbade the unnecessary destruction of civilian property or loss of civilian lives. For U.S. soldiers, however, it was often unclear who was a civilian and who was a guerrilla. If U.S. Army patrols suffered a steady stream of casualties from sniper fire or booby-trap bombs in a particular area, the response was often to create a "free-fire zone." U.S. soldiers ordered the local people to collect their belongings

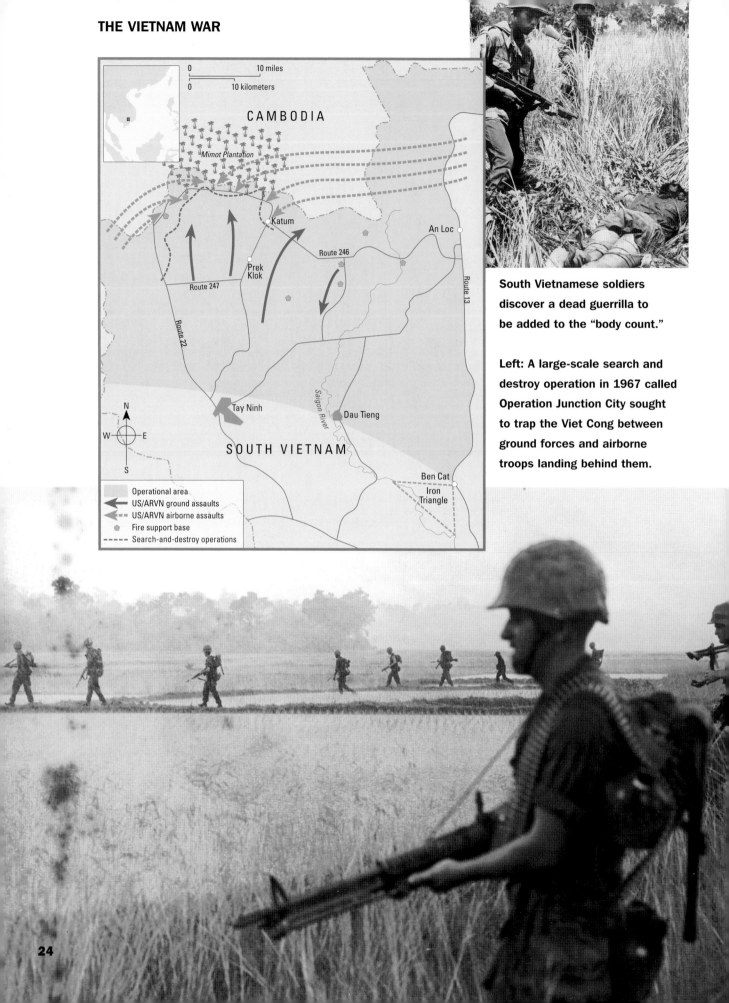

Map labels:

0 — 10 miles
0 — 10 kilometers

CAMBODIA

Mimot Plantation

Katum

An Loc

Route 246

Prek
Klok

Route 247

Route 22

Route 13

N
W — E
S

Tay Ninh

Saigon River

Dau Tieng

SOUTH VIETNAM

Ben Cat
Iron
Triangle

Operational area
US/ARVN ground assaults
US/ARVN airborne assaults
Fire support base
Search-and-destroy operations

South Vietnamese soldiers discover a dead guerrilla to be added to the "body count."

Left: A large-scale search and destroy operation in 1967 called Operation Junction City sought to trap the Viet Cong between ground forces and airborne troops landing behind them.

and leave, and any person who stayed in the free-fire zone could be regarded as Viet Cong and treated accordingly. Even when peasants were not deliberately driven out of their villages, they often fled their homes when an area became a battlefield. Some 1.5 million South Vietnamese were thought to be living in refugee camps by the end of 1967.

COUNTRYWIDE CONFLICT By that time, the number of U.S. military personnel committed to South Vietnam was approaching a half million. They were fighting from the Mekong Delta in the south— where the U.S. Army and Navy worked together to make aggressive pushes up various rivers in guerrilla territory—to areas near the North Vietnamese border, where U.S. military outposts came under attack from the NVA. Whenever U.S. forces succeeded in engaging the enemy, they won the fight. But they could never achieve a victory that was in any sense decisive.

Operation Junction City, which took place from February to April 1967, showed clearly what could and could not be achieved. The operation involved more than 25,000 U.S. and ARVN troops in an attempt to destroy NVA and Viet Cong bases near the Cambodian border. These forces overran the bases and killed approximately 2,800 enemy soldiers—about ten times the casualties the U.S. and ARVN forces suffered. But they were unable to occupy the area permanently, and enemy operations were only briefly disrupted.

Looking for solid evidence of progress in the war, the U.S. government settled for "body counts"— regularly updated figures of guerrillas killed in action. Although these figures were undoubtedly exaggerated, they did show the damage that U.S. forces were able to inflict on the Viet Cong and NVA. The communists never lost their will to fight, however, and the body count that mattered more to the future of the war was that of American lives lost. By the end of 1967, about 16,000 U.S. servicemen had been killed in Vietnam. The ultimate question was, how long would Americans back home go on accepting these losses? The answer came in 1968.

Opposite page, bottom: U.S. Marines advance through a rice field during a search and destroy operation in 1967. U.S. soldiers in rural South Vietnam had to be constantly on the watch for snipers or for mines that could kill or maim.

NOT A PRETTY PICTURE

By 1967, U.S. defense secretary Robert McNamara had become disillusioned with the Vietnam War. Before he resigned his post in the fall of that year, McNamara stated: *"The picture of the world's greatest superpower killing or seriously injuring 1,000 non-combatants a week, while trying to pound a tiny backward nation into submission . . . is not a pretty one."*
—Quoted in *The Ten Thousand Day War*, Michael Maclear

U.S. troops rush a wounded soldier to a waiting helicopter. The speed with which helicopters could evacuate casualties helped save thousands of lives.

CHAPTER 4
A TURNING POINT: 1968

U.S. airborne troops prepare to board a helicopter at a landing zone near Khe Sanh in April 1968.

Below: From January to April 1968, the U.S. Marine base at Khe Sanh was besieged by about 40,000 NVA troops.

By the start of 1968, the North Vietnamese leadership had decided that the time was ripe for a final push to drive U.S. forces out of South Vietnam. The Viet Cong and NVA began preparations for a coordinated offensive to take over towns and cities throughout the country. Ho Chi Minh and other North Vietnamese leaders expected that the communists would be welcomed as liberators in urban areas, and that mass desertions would lead to the collapse of the South Vietnamese army.

KHE SANH As a prelude to this offensive, on January 21, 1968, about 40,000 NVA troops laid siege to Khe Sanh, a base in the far north of South Vietnam that held about

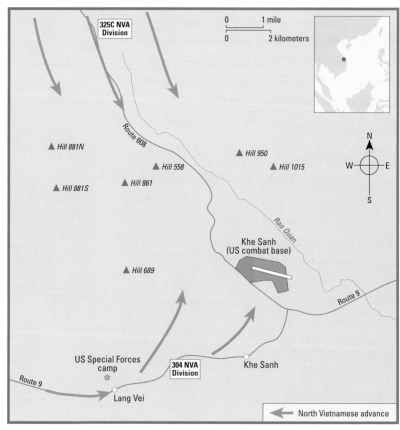

5,000 U.S. Marines. The U.S. military was determined to avoid the kind of defeat the French suffered at Dien Bien Phu. The besieged base was supplied by air, and round-the-clock air attacks, including heavy bombing by B-52s, battered the NVA troops dug in around the base. Although U.S. Marines were pounded by NVA rocket and artillery fire, they held firm during 77 days of fighting. On April 8, a relief column of U.S. forces broke through to Khe Sanh, lifting the siege.

TET OFFENSIVE The communists launched their major offensive at the end of January, with the start of the Vietnamese Tet national holiday. At this time, many soldiers in the South Vietnamese army were on leave, so the army would not be prepared to fight. After some preliminary attacks on January 30, the Tet offensive began in earnest on the night of January 31. About 85,000 communist fighters attacked more than 100 cities and towns in South Vietnam. Except for the northern regions of the country, where NVA troops played a leading role, most of the communists were Viet Cong guerrillas.

The offensive, which took the U.S. Army and ARVN by surprise, initially achieved many of its

U.S. soldiers hurry to board a helicopter during the operation to break the siege of Khe Sanh in April 1968.

Two South Vietnamese soldiers take part in the fight against communist guerrillas in Saigon during the Tet offensive in January 1968.

Viet Cong guerrillas, captured by South Vietnamese troops, kneel blindfolded in a Saigon street, February 1968.

objectives. In Saigon, communist guerrillas broke into the U.S. embassy compound and larger forces attacked other key military and political installations in the city. NVA forces, meanwhile, occupied Hue, Vietnam's former imperial capital.

But there was no uprising of local people in support of the communists, and the ARVN did not collapse—instead, it performed far better than expected. Mounting counterattacks, ARVN and U.S.

forces soon recaptured most urban areas, and they cleared Saigon of communists within a week. Only Hue was held by the communists for a prolonged period before it was retaken.

Militarily, Tet was a disaster for the Viet Cong and, to a lesser degree, the NVA. About 30,000 communists died in the first two weeks of February 1968, compared with about 3,000 deaths for the U.S. Army, the ARVN, and their allies. Fighting in the first half of

A MILITARY PARADOX

During the Tet offensive, one U.S. major involved in retaking the Mekong Delta town of Ben Tre from the Viet Cong allegedly told an interviewer:
"We had to destroy the town in order to save it."
　　　—Quoted in *Guerrilla Warfare,* Robin Corbett

1968 more or less destroyed the Viet Cong guerrilla movement, and the war had to be carried on largely by the NVA.

The political impact of the Tet offensive, however, was disastrous

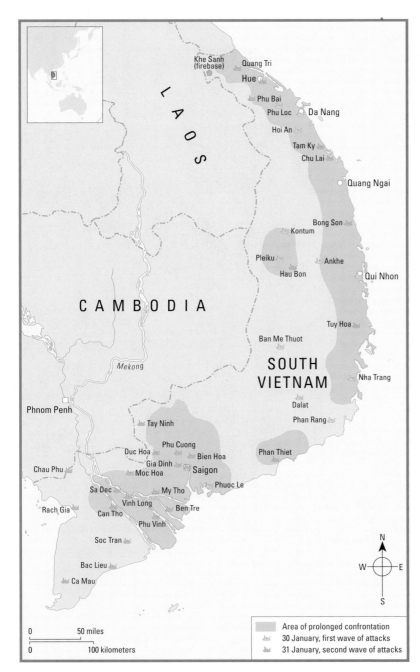

Left: During the Tet offensive at the end of January 1968, communist forces attacked towns and cities across South Vietnam.

Above: Folk singer Joan Baez, one of the most prominent celebrity antiwar campaigners, takes part in a protest rally in New York.

Map labels: Khe Sanh (firebase), Quang Tri, Hue, Phu Bai, Phu Loc, Da Nang, Hoi An, Tam Ky, Chu Lai, Quang Ngai, Bong Son, Kontum, Pleiku, Ankhe, Hau Bon, Qui Nhon, Tuy Hoa, Ban Me Thuot, SOUTH VIETNAM, Nha Trang, Dalat, Phan Rang, Tay Ninh, Phu Cuong, Phan Thiet, Duc Hoa, Gia Dinh, Bien Hoa, Chau Phu, Moc Hoa, Saigon, Phnom Penh, Sa Dec, My Tho, Phuoc Le, Vinh Long, Ben Tre, Rach Gia, Can Tho, Phu Vinh, Soc Tran, Bac Lieu, Ca Mau, LAOS, CAMBODIA, Mekong

0   50 miles
0   100 kilometers

Area of prolonged confrontation
30 January, first wave of attacks
31 January, second wave of attacks

for the U.S. government. There had been an antiwar movement in the United States since the very start of the Vietnam conflict. It drew the support of many college students, as well as prominent individuals such as civil rights leader Martin Luther King, Jr. Antiwar protesters believed the United States was fighting against a popular liberation movement and doing so in a particularly brutal way. Protests ranged from large-scale demonstrations to the burning of draft cards—given to men eligible to be drafted into the armed services—and individual refusal to be drafted.

People who were prosecuted for refusing the draft included world boxing champion Muhammad Ali.

Until the Tet offensive, however, the majority of U.S. citizens had continued to support the war effort, if with mounting doubts. Then, after almost three years of large-scale commitment of U.S. forces, the American public saw the effects of the Tet offensive on their televisions, with fighting in the streets of South Vietnam's cities and even outside the U.S. embassy. Inevitably, public confidence in the chances of success in the war was severely shaken.

Unknown to the public, the U.S. government had also lost confidence in winning the war. After Tet, with the siege of Khe Sanh and the battle for Hue still

U.S. Marines in action during street fighting in Hue in spring 1968. About 1,000 Marines were killed or wounded in the battle to retake the city from the NVA.

onward, the United States no longer sought victory. Instead, it looked for a way out of the conflict.

The destruction wrought upon South Vietnam during 1968—shown in graphic detail on televised news programs in the United States and other parts of the world—made for a disturbing spectacle. In Hue, U.S. Marines and Army soldiers, aided by the ARVN, fought for more than three weeks to retake the city from the NVA. House-to-house fighting, plus shelling by U.S. warships, reduced large parts of the city to rubble. The noncombatant (not involved in fighting) dead in Hue included at least 2,800 South Vietnamese government officials, military officers, and others rounded up and massacred by the communists.

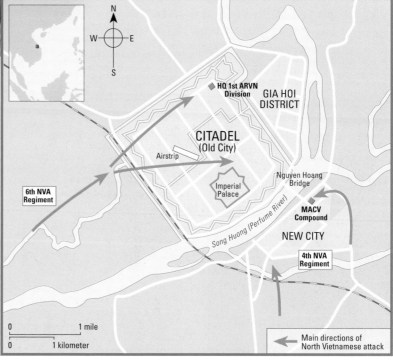

raging, General Westmoreland requested the commitment of another 200,000 U.S. troops to Vietnam. With these extra soldiers— and permission to invade Cambodia and Laos to cut communist supply lines—Westmoreland insisted he could win the war. But a report by U.S. defense secretary Clark Clifford concluded that, "All that can be said is that additional troops would enable us to kill more of the enemy …"

FINDING A WAY OUT
The year 1968 was a presidential election year in the United States. On March 31, 1968, President Lyndon Johnson announced that he would not stand for re-election. At the same time, the Rolling Thunder bombing raids on North Vietnam were scaled down and the United States sought to open peace negotiations. From that point

On January 31, 1968, NVA troops attacked the city of Hue. They occupied the Citadel, or old city, apart from ARVN headquarters, and they threatened the MACV Compound, the U.S. headquarters. It took 24 days to retake the Citadel from the NVA.

In 1968, almost 15,000 U.S. servicemen were killed in action in Vietnam—nearly 300 a week. Constantly on the lookout for potential enemies, some U.S. soldiers began to view all Vietnamese people with suspicion and hostility. This fact was laid bare on

March 16, 1968, when one of the most notorious atrocities of the war took place. On that day, U.S. soldiers massacred more than 300 South Vietnamese civilians, including women and children, from the hamlet of My Lai. A number of soldiers were later prosecuted for their part in the killings, and one soldier, Lieutenant William Calley, was convicted.

The war dominated the 1968 U.S. presidential election, with violent clashes erupting between antiwar demonstrators and police at the Democratic party convention in Chicago. In November, Republican Richard M. Nixon won the election. He had promised both to "get tough with the communists" and "bring our boys back home."

By then the United States had taken steps toward withdrawing troops from Vietnam. In June 1968, Westmoreland, his request for more troops denied, was replaced by General Creighton W. Abrams as U.S. commander in Vietnam. At the end of October, the bombing of North Vietnam halted. Peace talks were scheduled to begin at the start of 1969. A new phase of the war had begun.

GETTING OUT OF VIETNAM

American author William Broyles Jr., who served as a Marine in Vietnam, wrote:
"There was no single goal in Vietnam; there were 2.8 million goals, one for every American who served there. And in the end the nation's goal became what each soldier's had been all along: to get out of Vietnam."
—From *Brothers in Arms*, William Broyles

A man lies dead in Hue. The Vietnam conflict was the first televised war, and scenes such as this one, shown on televisions across the United States, helped fuel antiwar sentiment.

VIETNAMIZATION: 1969–1971

U.S. soldiers cross a river in the A Shau Valley, rugged country ideal for guerrilla operations.

Despite the shocks of the siege of Khe Sanh and the Tet offensive, in the second half of 1968 and the start of 1969 the war went on much as before. U.S. troops continued to carry out major offensive operations to seek out and destroy the enemy. Such operations only came to an end after the battle of the A Shau Valley in May 1969.

The battle began on May 10, when the U.S. 101st Airborne Division flew in by helicopter to take on North Vietnamese troops dug in on the slopes of a hill in the valley, which was close to the border with Laos. A fierce battle began as the airborne division, soon backed up by other U.S. and ARVN troops, assaulted the NVA positions. The hill was soon nicknamed Hamburger Hill, because of the number of soldiers chewed up on its slopes.

On May 20, U.S. and ARVN forces overran the NVA positions—a clear military victory. But the battle for Hamburger Hill caused an outcry in the United States. The U.S. casualties had been 46 dead and some 400 wounded. Earlier in the war, the American public might have considered such losses acceptable. In 1969, however, they were widely regarded as unacceptably high. U.S. soldiers had also begun to lose their will to fight. At this point in the war, morale in many units of the U.S. Army in Vietnam went into sharp decline. Many soldiers had no desire to risk their lives for what was widely regarded as a lost cause.

After Hamburger Hill, the U.S. government, with President Richard Nixon now in charge, ordered General Abrams to avoid any further large-scale battles in Vietnam. In June 1969, Nixon announced the first U.S. troop withdrawals from the country. He declared it a priority that the ARVN forces should take over the prime combat role in the war. This policy was known as "Vietnamization."

the ARVN into an efficient fighting force. When Abrams took over from Westmoreland as head of U.S. forces in Vietnam in 1968, measures were already being taken to expand ARVN troop numbers rapidly and improve their equipment.

At the same time, South Vietnam had found a man who could provide real leadership. General Nguyen Van Thieu had emerged as the most capable of the South Vietnamese generals who vied for power in the mid-1960s. In September 1967, Thieu became president of South Vietnam after an election that was, by South Vietnamese standards, reasonably free and fair. Although labeled a "puppet" of the United States by the communists and the

Richard M. Nixon was U.S president from 1969 to 1974.

In a sense, there was nothing new about this policy. From the start of its involvement in Vietnam, the United States' official aim had been to make South Vietnam into a self-sustaining and independent country, capable of defending itself. Once U.S. troops began pouring into the country in 1965, this goal had become largely overlooked as the United States concentrated on direct military confrontation. But back in mid-1967, General Abrams had been given the task of turning

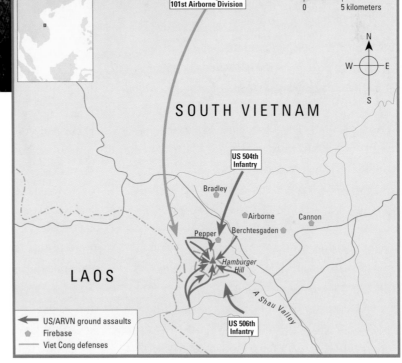

On May 10, 1969, troops of the U.S. 101st Airborne were flown into the A Shau Valley, where they engaged the NVA on Hamburger Hill. After reinforcements were brought in, the hill was captured on May 20.

A U.S. soldier holds a gun to the head of a
Vietnamese peasant woman. Photos like this helped
persuade many that the war in Vietnam was wrong.

U.S. antiwar movement, Thieu proved a leader of
independent spirit who pursued what he regarded
as South Vietnam's best interests.

Along with trying to build up the ARVN, the
U.S. military and the South Vietnamese government
made progress with "pacification"—a policy that
sought to eliminate the communist organization in
rural South Vietnam and put the country more
securely under government control. The main group
behind the pacification effort was Civil Operations
and Revolutionary Development Support, or CORDS,
in which the U.S. Central Intelligence Agency, or CIA,
played a leading role. Beginning in the summer of
1968, the pacification campaign had increasing success.
In many areas, refugees were resettled and local pro-
government militias took responsibility for keeping
their villages secure. A land reform program sought to
distribute land to peasants, helping to win their "hearts
and minds." At the same time, through the ruthless
"Phoenix" program (which also involved the CIA),
thousands of communist activists in South Vietnam
were identified and either arrested or killed.

Ironically, by the second half of 1969, when
support for the war among the American public was
evaporating, the security situation in South Vietnam
had vastly improved. Fighting went on mostly in areas
close to the border with Cambodia and Laos, away

Right: By 1971, most densely populated areas in South Vietnam had been brought firmly under government control, and fighting with communist forces took place largely in border areas.

Below: U.S. Marines cross the Vu Gia river in pursuit of communist forces in June 1969. By that time, such offensive operations were being phased out because they cost too many U.S. lives.

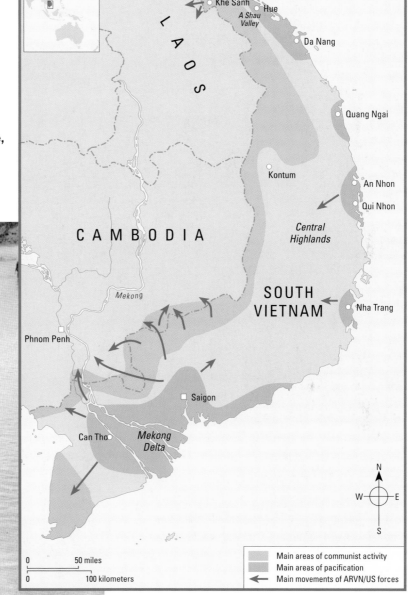

Main areas of communist activity
Main areas of pacification
→ Main movements of ARVN/US forces

from major population centers. Heavy losses among South Vietnamese communists, especially from the Tet offensive and as a result of the Phoenix program, had mostly ended the insurgency in South Vietnam. The South Vietnamese government had secure control of large areas of the countryside. In North Vietnam, the death of Ho Chi Minh in September 1969 deprived the communists of a national leader of great stature.

Between the second half of 1969 and the spring of 1972, the amount of combat in Vietnam was much lower than in the previous four years. U.S. troop levels

Young North Vietnamese soldiers captured during the incursion into Cambodia in 1970.

fell steadily as Nixon fulfilled his promise to "bring the boys home." But the troop withdrawals did not mean the president was prepared to accept a communist victory in Vietnam. While scaling down the troop numbers, Nixon simultaneously widened the war. In March 1969, he secretly authorized the bombing of North Vietnamese bases in Cambodia.

CAMBODIA Since gaining independence from the French, Cambodia had been ruled by Prince Norodom Sihanouk. He tried to keep his country free of involvement in the war in Vietnam, but this policy meant turning a blind eye to North Vietnamese bases and supply lines in Cambodia. The United States government put pressure on Sihanouk to crack down on the communist presence in Cambodia. Then, in March 1970, while Sihanouk was out of the country, he was overthrown in a coup led by Lon Nol, a pro-U.S. Cambodian general.

BUYING TIME

When U.S. and ARVN forces made an incursion into Cambodia in 1970, the main goal was to postpone a major NVA offensive until the ARVN was in a fit condition to defend South Vietnam. President Nixon declared:

"We have bought time for the South Vietnamese to strengthen themselves against the enemy."
—Quoted in *Historical Atlas of the Vietnam War*, Harry Summers Jr. and Stanley Karnow

The bombing and the political instability in Cambodia created a dangerous situation. There were fears that the NVA might attack the Cambodian capital, Phnom Penh. Cambodia also had its own communist guerrilla movement, the Khmer Rouge, which was a growing threat to the government. At the end of April 1970, Nixon authorized U.S. and ARVN troops to cross from South Vietnam into Cambodia. These incursions, aimed at communist bases, were intended to relieve communist pressure on Phnom Penh and to disrupt NVA preparations for a major attack against South Vietnam. The two main targets were known as Parrot's Beak and Fish Hook. About 25,000 ARVN and U.S. troops, with powerful air support, pushed 18 miles (30 km) inside Cambodia, where they overran communist bases and seized large quantities of arms and ammunition.

The incursion into Cambodia provoked a wave of antiwar protests across the United States, including demonstrations at Kent State University in Ohio. On May 4, 1970, National Guardsmen shot demonstrators at the university, killing four and wounding eleven. The incursion also brought about a hostile reaction from Congress, which repealed the Gulf of Tonkin Resolution (*see page 14*) and ordered the president to withdraw U.S. troops from Cambodia by the end of June. In December 1970, Congress banned any further use of U.S. ground troops beyond the borders of South Vietnam. When an incursion into Laos was carried out from January to March 1971, to attack NVA bases and the Ho Chi Minh Trail, only ARVN troops took part, with the support of U.S. aircraft and long-range artillery. The "Vietnamization" of the war had taken place.

A student antiwar protester is shot dead at Kent State University in May 1970.

Map

N W E S

CAMBODIA

Snoul

The City

Mimot Route 7

Fish Hook

An Loc

Route 22

SOUTH VIETNAM

Route 13

Tay Ninh

Saigon River

Route 1

Parrot's Beak

SAIGON

0 ——— 10 miles
0 ——— 10 kilometers

◀— US/ARVN ground assaults
◀-- US/ARVN airborne assaults
(H) Helicopter landing zone
⬬ Suspected communist headquarters

In April to May 1970, U.S. and ARVN forces crossed from South Vietnam into Cambodia to attack communist bases. The main targets were areas named Parrot's Beak and Fish Hook.

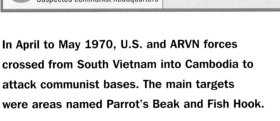

CHAPTER 6
EASTER OFFENSIVE TO CHRISTMAS BOMBING

President Nixon (foreground, right) visits Beijing, China, in February 1972. By normalizing relations with China, Nixon threatened North Vietnam with the potential loss of Chinese support.

Cheerful U.S. Marines embark on the journey home from South Vietnam in March 1971. About 150,000 U.S. soldiers were left in Vietnam by that year's end.

By the start of 1972, peace talks between the warring sides in Vietnam had been under way for three years. The negotiations, held in Paris, involved representatives of the United States, the South Vietnamese and North Vietnamese governments, and the communist Provisional Revolutionary Government of South Vietnam, or PRG. There were also secret meetings between U.S. national security adviser Henry Kissinger and the head of the North Vietnamese delegation at the talks, Le Duc Tho. But neither public nor secret negotiations brought any progress toward ending the fighting.

There was, however, diplomatic progress on the wider world stage.

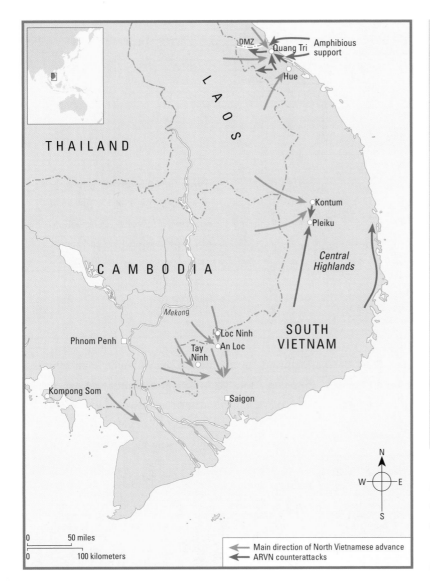

THAILAND

L A O S

DMZ
Quang Tri · Amphibious support
Hue

Kontum
Pleiku

Central Highlands

C A M B O D I A

Mekong

SOUTH
VIETNAM

Phnom Penh

Loc Ninh
An Loc
Tay Ninh

Kompong Som

Saigon

N
W—E
S

| 0 | 50 miles |
| 0 | 100 kilometers |

←— Main direction of North Vietnamese advance
←— ARVN counterattacks

RETREAT FROM QUANG TRI

A German journalist witnessed the disorganized retreat of South Vietnamese soldiers after the fall of Quang Tri City in May 1972: *"Around noon the first bunch of fleeing soldiers started arriving at the May Chanh bridge. . . . Some were drunk and kept firing wildly into the air. The line of lorries and army vehicles roared on south as if the devil himself were at their heels."*

—Quoted in *Death in the Ricefields*, Peter Scholl-Latour

During the NVA's 1972 Easter offensive, the fighting raged around Quang Tri in the north, Kontum in the Central Highlands, and An Loc on the road to Saigon.

President Nixon had undertaken a bold initiative to improve relations between the United States and the two major communist powers, China and the Soviet Union. In February 1972, Nixon became the first U.S. president to visit communist China. North Vietnam depended on these two communist powers for arms supplies and diplomatic support, and if they grew more friendly with the United States, North Vietnam risked being isolated. This risk probably influenced North Vietnam's decision to take a military gamble.

General Vo Nguyen Giap, the North Vietnamese minister of defense, had long been known as a master of guerrilla warfare. But by 1972 he believed the time was ripe to try a new military strategy. With fewer than 100,000 U.S. military personnel left in South Vietnam

and more troop withdrawals planned, there was no possibility that U.S. ground forces would be committed again to major fighting. The defense of South Vietnam —on the ground, at least—was therefore in the hands of the ARVN, an army that the North Vietnamese believed they could beat. General Giap planned a full-scale invasion of South Vietnam by NVA forces, using tanks and heavy artillery in support of large troop formations.

The NVA offensive began on March 30, 1972, which was Good Friday, and for this reason it is often known as the Easter, or Eastertide, offensive. Giap distributed his 130,000 troops on three lines of attack. The offensive opened with a push into Quang Tri Province, immediately south of the demilitarized

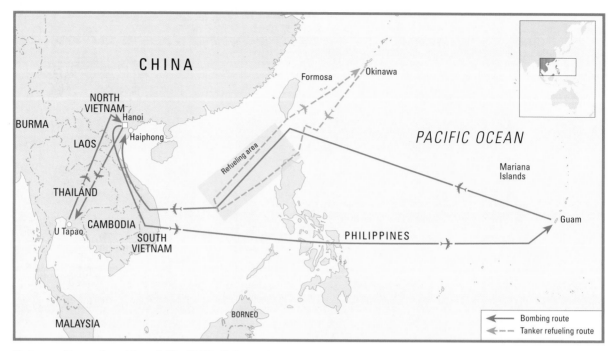

Between December 18 and 29, 1972, U.S. B-52 bombers carried out intensive raids chiefly against targets in the North Vietnamese cities of Hanoi and Haiphong, dropping about 22,000 tons of bombs in total. The B-52s based on Guam required in-flight refueling to achieve the round trip. Other bombers flew from the U Tapao base in Thailand.

zone, or DMZ, separating North and South Vietnam. In early April, the NVA struck toward An Loc north of Saigon. Later that month, another front was opened in the Central Highlands with a thrust toward Kontum.

U.S. and South Vietnamese military commanders had expected a major North Vietnamese attack since the previous year. They had observed the buildup of troops and supplies. But they had been unable to predict the exact timing of the offensive and were largely caught off guard. In places, the NVA's use of tanks and long-range artillery caused the South Vietnamese defenders to retreat in near panic. On each of the three fronts, the NVA made gains. By April 13, the North Vietnamese had put An Loc under siege and were advancing toward Saigon, eventually coming

South Vietnamese soldiers stand near the bodies of two enemies killed north of Quang Tri in April 1972. Communist losses in the Easter offensive were heavy.

within 40 miles (65 km) of the capital. Quang Tri City fell to the NVA on May 1. By then Kontum was also under threat, raising the prospect of the NVA advancing down to the coast and cutting the country in two. The sight of South Vietnamese soldiers and civilian refugees fleeing south from Quang Tri City seemed about to herald the collapse of South Vietnam.

LINEBACKER RAIDS

The United States responded to the offensive by resuming its bombing campaign against North Vietnam. The new campaign was code-named Linebacker, and it began in April. Having switched from guerrilla to conventional warfare, the NVA now required far more supplies to keep the war in the South going. The Linebacker raids struck at North Vietnam's entire supply chain, including not only roads, bridges, and railways but also fuel depots, ammunition dumps, and warehouses in cities. (Most controversially, the entrances to North Vietnamese ports were mined to prevent supplies arriving by sea from the Soviet Union.) Linebacker was more effective than Rolling Thunder had been, partly because U.S. aircraft used the first laser-guided "smart" bombs, which were highly accurate, and partly because the air operations did not have as many politically imposed restrictions on targeting.

Rescuers search for survivors in the rubble of a Hanoi hospital destroyed by a bomb during the Linebacker 2 raids, December 1972. The bomb had been meant for a nearby barracks.

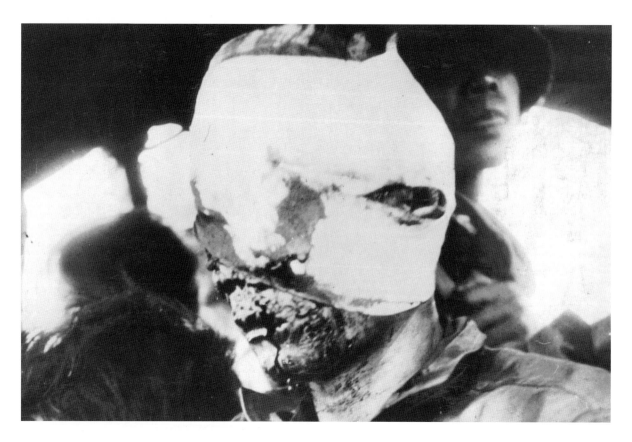

A wounded ARVN soldier. Many South Vietnamese who had fought hard against the communists felt betrayed by the 1973 Paris peace agreement, which resulted in U.S. forces pulling out of the war.

The impact of the Linebacker raids was one factor that contributed to a turn of the tide in the war during May 1972. The performance of the ARVN improved after President Thieu replaced some incompetent generals with better commanders and sent better motivated units to hold key positions. U.S. and South Vietnamese airpower played a decisive role in support of the ground forces, with a variety of strike aircraft, gunships, attack helicopters, and bombers hammering the North Vietnamese troops. At An Loc in the second week of May, for example, flights of B-52 bombers struck NVA positions every 55 minutes for almost 30 hours. Along the coast around Quang Tri, firepower from the air was supplemented by the guns of U.S. warships stationed offshore.

The NVA's progress slowed and then halted. An NVA assault on Kontum was driven back at the end of May, and by mid-June the siege of An Loc had been lifted. An ARVN counter-offensive retook Quang Tri City in mid-September. NVA forces typically fought with remarkable determination under the awesome barrage of bombs, shells, and napalm to which they were subjected. But their losses of men and equipment were severe. According to some estimates, about 100,000 NVA troops were killed between March and October 1972—more than double the losses on the South Vietnamese side. Yet the offensive still left the NVA in possession of significant areas of South Vietnamese territory.

U.S. BOMBING OF NORTH VIETNAM 1972

Linebacker 1 (April–October 1972)

Bombs dropped	172,000 tons
U.S. aircraft lost	44

Linebacker 2 (December 1972)

Bombs dropped	22,000 tons
U.S. aircraft lost	26 (including 15 B-52s)

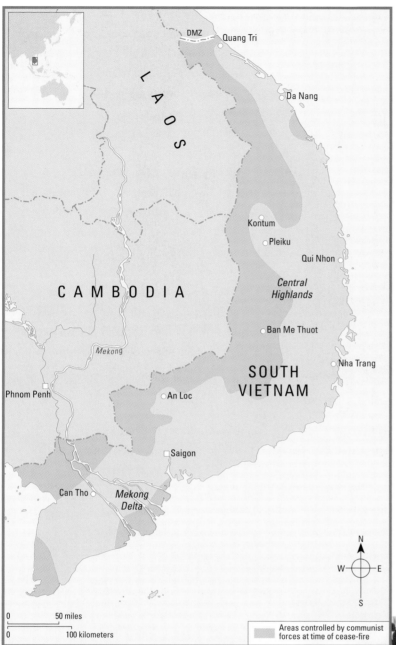

DMZ
Quang Tri

L A O S

Da Nang

Kontum
Pleiku
Qui Nhon

Central
Highlands

C A M B O D I A

Ban Me Thuot

Mekong

Nha Trang

SOUTH
VIETNAM

Phnom Penh

An Loc

Saigon

Can Tho   Mekong
Delta

N
W — E
S

0   50 miles
0   100 kilometers

Areas controlled by communist
forces at time of cease-fire

once more stalled, Nixon ordered the bombing of North Vietnam on an unprecedented scale. Between December 18 and 30, a series of raids by B-52s—more than 100 bombers at a time—destroyed almost every target of any military value in Hanoi and Haiphong. Code-named Linebacker 2, this "Christmas bombing" killed about 1,600 civilians.

In January 1973, peace talks resumed. Agreement was soon reached on terms almost identical to those on the table before the Christmas bombing. A peace deal was formally signed on January 27. For the United States, the war in Vietnam was over.

The 1973 peace agreement allowed NVA forces to stay in occupation of areas of South Vietnam that they had seized in the Easter offensive.

Henry Kissinger (facing camera, center) signs the Paris peace agreement on behalf of the United States, January 27, 1973.

PEACE TREATY

PEACE TREATY The Linebacker raids stopped on October 22, 1972. Shortly after, it was announced that the United States and North Vietnam had reached an agreement in principle on a peace deal. The United States would pull its forces out of Vietnam, but North Vietnamese forces would be allowed to stay in their positions in South Vietnam. In return, the North Vietnamese accepted that President Thieu would, for the time being, remain in power in Saigon.

A signed peace agreement, however, proved far from easy to accomplish. In mid-December, with talks

CHAPTER 7
COMMUNISM TRIUMPHS

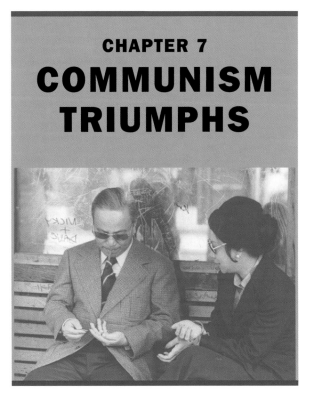

aSouth Vietnamese president Nguyen Van Thieu—photographed here with his wife—knew that his country's fate depended on continuing U.S. support, both financial and military.

U.S. prisoners of war are freed by their North Vietnamese captors at Gia Lam airport, Hanoi, in 1973, in accordance with the terms of the Paris peace agreement.

U.S. national security adviser Henry Kissinger and North Vietnamese negotiator Le Duc Tho were jointly awarded the Nobel Peace Prize for their efforts in achieving the 1973 peace agreement. Le Duc Tho, however, declined to accept the award, on the grounds that there was no peace. The agreement, in reality, merely opened a new phase of the war. ARVN and NVA forces were fighting small-scale local battles in the week that the agreement was signed.

President Thieu had been very reluctant to sign the peace accord. He felt that an agreement that left 150,000 North Vietnamese troops within his country's borders amounted to a sellout. Thieu obtained a written assurance from President Nixon that the United States would intervene militarily in support of South Vietnam if the North Vietnamese broke the peace agreement by resuming major offensive action. So, although the last U.S. troops pulled out of Vietnam in March 1973, South Vietnam remained dependent for its survival on U.S. financial aid and the promise of U.S. military intervention.

TESTING RESOLVE

Gerald Ford, who succeeded Richard Nixon as U.S. president in August 1974, was regarded by the North Vietnamese as a weak leader. A North Vietnamese journalist wrote:
"We tested Ford's resolve by attacking Phuoc Long in January 1975. When Ford kept American B-52s in their hangars, our leadership decided on a big offensive against South Vietnam."
—Quoted in *Historical Atlas of the Vietnam War*, Harry Summers Jr. and Stanley Karnow

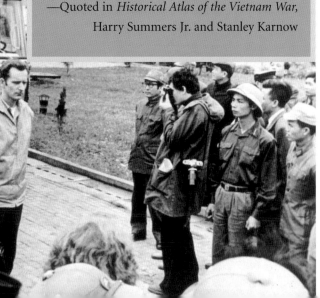

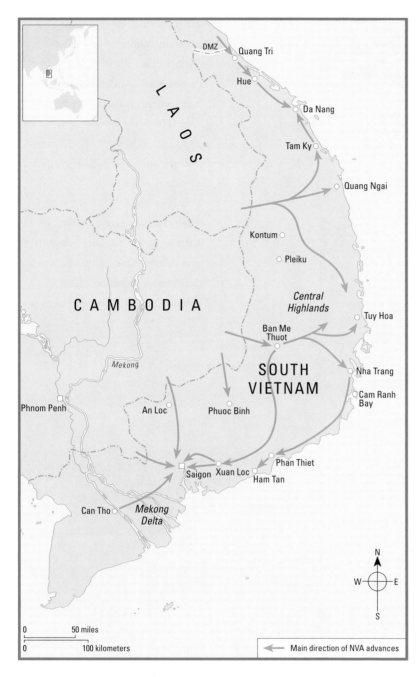

The NVA's victorious offensive, from March to April 1975, began with a breakthrough in the Central Highlands, followed by the seizure of the north and a final drive on Saigon.

0   50 miles
0   100 kilometers

← Main direction of NVA advances

then, Nixon was embroiled in the Watergate political scandal, which involved a break-in at Democratic headquarters during the 1972 presidential election campaign and a subsequent coverup. The scandal would lead to Nixon's resignation in August 1974.

In Vietnam, meanwhile, the balance of power gradually shifted. For most of 1973, the ARVN had the upper hand. U.S. arms rushed in during the period before the peace agreement meant that the South Vietnamese were substantially better equipped than their enemy. The North Vietnamese, for their part, took time to recover both from their losses in the fighting of 1972 and from the damage caused by the U.S. Linebacker bombing campaigns.

At the end of 1973, however, the balance of power began to move decisively in favor of North Vietnam. While the Soviet Union increased its aid to North Vietnam, the U.S. Congress cut aid to South

It soon became clear that the United States could not be relied upon to fulfill its promises to South Vietnam. The U.S. Congress, reflecting the mood of the American people, was not receptive to any continued military involvement in Southeast Asia. In August 1973, a Congressional vote halted the bombing of Cambodia, which had continued after the pullout from Vietnam. The following November, a War Powers Resolution banned the president from sending U.S. forces into action without the prior approval of Congress. By

Vietnam. The United States had built up the ARVN into an American-style army, reliant on sophisticated armaments and "gas-guzzling" vehicles. As money ran short, the South Vietnamese forces could not afford the spare parts, ammunition, and fuel to keep their war machine running.

During 1974, the fighting, although still localized, grew in scale. Some 31,000 ARVN troops were killed in action that year. The North Vietnamese, meanwhile, transformed the jungle tracks of the Ho Chi Minh

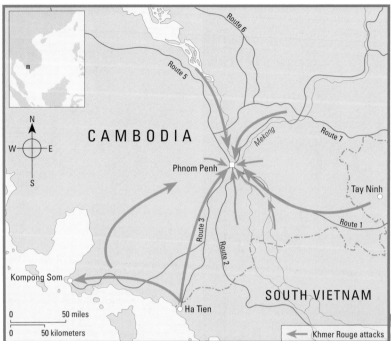

In Cambodia, Khmer Rouge guerrillas advanced from all sides to take the capital, Phnom Penh, which fell to the communists on April 17, 1975.

South Vietnamese civilians, desperate to escape the fighting near Xuan Loc in April 1975, struggle to board an ARVN Chinook helicopter as it takes off.

Trail into a paved road, down which soldiers and supplies poured into their zones in South Vietnam. They even built an oil pipeline into the South to keep their vehicles supplied with fuel.

PUSH FOR VICTORY In December 1974, the North Vietnamese decided to seek a final military victory. Only U.S. intervention would have deterred them—the Easter offensive had taught them that they could not take over South Vietnam in the face of U.S airpower. But in January 1975, when NVA troops seized a South Vietnamese provincial capital, Phuoc Binh, the United States did nothing. North Vietnamese leaders concluded that they could safely go ahead with the conquest of South Vietnam.

Commanded by General Van Tien Dung, who had taken over from General Giap, the NVA began the final offensive in the beginning of March 1975. The main thrust of the attack was through the Central Highlands toward the coast. Poorly led and demoralized, the ARVN forces rapidly disintegrated. By the first week of April, the northern half of South Vietnam was under NVA control. Major cities such as Quang Tri and Hue

NVA soldiers on the balcony of the presidential palace in Saigon look down on North Vietnamese tanks parked in the palace grounds after the communist victory, April 30, 1975.

were abandoned by the ARVN with hardly a fight. Pushing south toward Saigon, the NVA forces met stiffer resistance, and it took them two weeks to overcome ARVN troops at Xuan Loc, north of the capital. But the ultimate outcome of the war was no longer in doubt.

On April 21, 1975, President Thieu resigned, denouncing the United States as a country that had "not honored its promises." An evacuation of Americans and selected South Vietnamese from Saigon turned into a race against time as the NVA closed in on the city. The last people to leave were lifted by helicopter from the roof

of the U.S. Embassy early on the morning of April 30. A few hours later, an NVA tank crashed through the gates of the South Vietnamese presidential palace.

Just a few days before the collapse of South Vietnam, Cambodia had likewise fallen to communist forces. The Khmer Rouge guerrillas had been within artillery range of the Cambodian capital, Phnom Penh, since early 1974. From the start of 1975, the besieged city was dependent on a U.S. airlift for essential supplies. The defensive perimeter of the city eventually crumbled after months of sustained pressure,

and on April 17, 1975, the Khmer Rouge marched into Phnom Penh as victors. By the end of 1975, when the communist Pathet Lao took power in Laos, all of former French Indochina—Vietnam, Cambodia, and Laos—was under communist rule.

CHAPTER 6
AFTERMATH

Left: The spraying of large areas of Vietnam with defoliants left a desolate landscape. It may also have caused long-term damage to local people's health.

Above: These skulls, belonging to Cambodian people killed by the Khmer Rouge, were found by the Vietnamese after they invaded Cambodia in 1979.

Many well-meaning antiwar campaigners in the United States and elsewhere had hoped that the communists in Indochina would behave reasonably after victory. These hopes had been encouraged during the war by the North Vietnamese leadership, who had talked of installing a coalition government in South Vietnam in which communists would share power with other Vietnamese nationalists. In fact, however, the two halves of Vietnam were swiftly united as the Socialist Republic of Vietnam under the same communist regime that had ruled North Vietnam. In a significant symbolic gesture, Saigon was renamed Ho Chi Minh City.

More than 200,000 former South Vietnamese officials and army officers were arrested after the communist victory and sent to "reeducation camps." Their treatment was mild, however, compared to what happened to the former enemies of the Khmer Rouge in Cambodia—now renamed Kampuchea. In that country, many thousands of supporters of the previous regime were killed. Almost the entire population of Phnom Penh was forcibly relocated to the countryside, where huge numbers died of disease,

ECOLOGICAL DAMAGE

The long-term damage caused to Vietnam by the spraying of defoliants has been a highly controversial issue. According to official U.S. figures:

Total area of Vietnam defoliated, 1962–1970	5,229,000 acres
Percentage of South Vietnamese forests sprayed, 1965–1971	46.4 percent
Percentage of South Vietnamese cultivated land sprayed, 1965–1971	3.2 percent

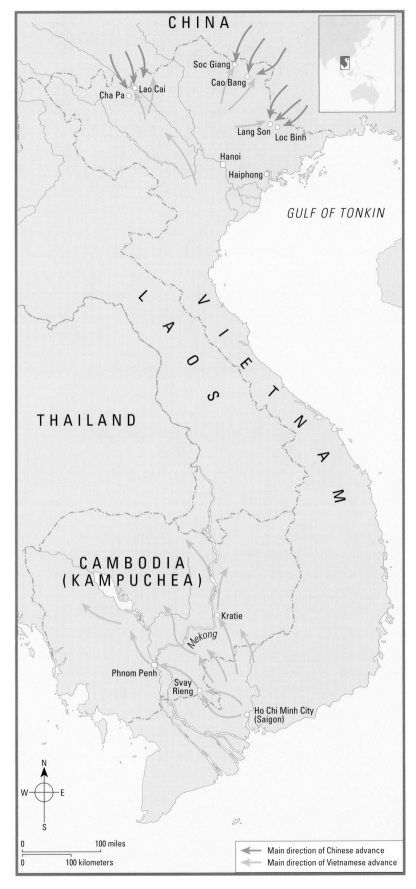

malnutrition, brutal treatment, or execution. Ultimately, between one and two million people died in the Cambodian "killing fields."

In former South Vietnam, people were also relocated from the cities to the countryside, although with less brutality than witnessed in Cambodia. Inevitably, life in rural areas was harsh. Mines had been scattered around the land, and the U.S. military had sprayed millions of acres with the chemical defoliant Agent Orange, which allegedly caused major, long-term health problems for inhabitants (as well as for U.S. veterans of the war). In southern cities, the departure of U.S. forces brought poverty to thousands of Vietnamese who had depended on them for their income. Communist economic policies then made matters worse by cracking down on private businesses. In the spring of 1978, thousands of people in Vietnam began to flee the country by sea. Many of these refugees, called "boat people," were ethnic Chinese who found themselves especially at odds with the communist regime.

If the aftermath of the Vietnam war was a shock to many Western antiwar campaigners, it also proved a surprise to those people, in the United States and elsewhere, who

In the winter of 1978–1979, Vietnamese forces invaded and occupied Cambodia (Kampuchea). China responded by invading Vietnam in February 1979, although the Chinese troops withdrew in March of that year.

Chinese troops direct artillery fire during China's border war with Vietnam in 1979.

had supported the war as a way to stop the expansion of communism. Communist China and Indochina did not form a united front and expand communism further across Asia. Instead, the communist countries in Asia turned to fighting one another.

NEW CONFLICTS

The Vietnamese had a long history of resistance to Chinese domination. There was also a tradition of hostility between the Khmers—the dominant ethnic group in Cambodia—and the Vietnamese. These tensions were mostly submerged during the war, but they resurfaced after U.S. forces pulled out.

In 1977, the Khmer Rouge began staging raids into Vietnam in places where the border was disputed. Low-level conflict rumbled on until Christmas 1978, when Vietnamese forces mounted a full-scale invasion of Cambodia. On January 7, 1979, they took Phnom Penh and installed a new government. Driven out of the cities, the Khmer Rouge returned to guerrilla warfare, harassing the Vietnamese from bases along the border with Thailand. Vietnamese forces stayed in Cambodia until 1989, when they withdrew to clear the way for a negotiated agreement on the country's future government.

The main backer of the Khmer Rouge regime in Cambodia was China. On February 17, 1979, Chinese troops invaded Vietnam. The Chinese did not want to conquer Vietnam. Instead, they sought to curb Vietnamese aggression. Chinese forces found it hard to make any progress against stiff resistance, however, and withdrew from Vietnam on March 6, 1979.

HOPE FOR THE FUTURE

These events left Vietnam solely reliant on the Soviet Union as a source of foreign aid. The collapse of communism in Eastern Europe in 1989, followed by the breakup of the Soviet Union in 1991, was a huge shock to Vietnam's leaders. Yet the 1990s brought improvement at last in the lives of many of the Vietnamese people. New economic policies, which encouraged free enterprise, revitalized Vietnam's cities. In 1995, relations with the United States were at last restored. Vietnam entered the new millennium still under the rule of the communist party and still extremely poor, especially in rural areas, but with increasing hope for the future.

By then, the United States had long emerged from the shadow cast by the Vietnam War. In the 1970s, the United States' self-confidence seemed to have been permanently dented by a conflict from which, for the first time in its history, it had not emerged victorious. But with the passage of time, the country's reluctance to use U.S. troops in conflicts abroad lessened. U.S. forces fought in the Gulf War in 1991, and they later fought in Afghanistan and Iraq. It seems unlikely, however, that the American people will ever again accept the level of casualties seen in Vietnam.

Today, more than 30 years after the 1973 peace agreement was signed, the Vietnam War has become history for a younger generation. For older people, the conflict is part of the living past, still vividly recalled. Vietnam has received a major source of income from the spending of American tourists, and many of them have been former soldiers revisiting the battlefields where they fought in their youth.

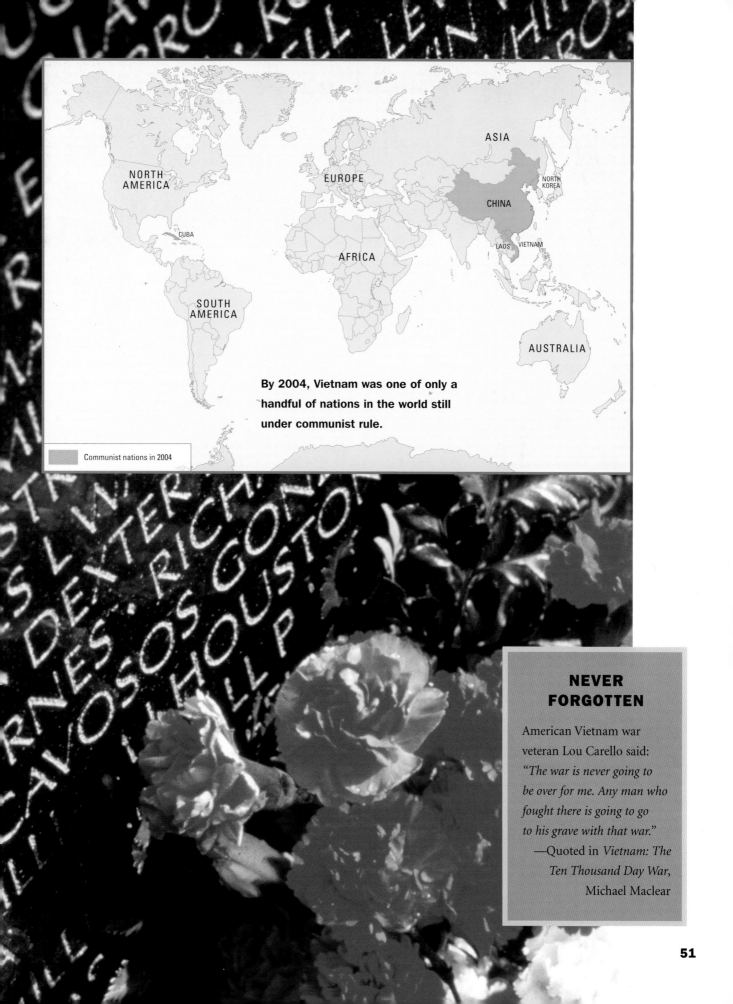

By 2004, Vietnam was one of only a handful of nations in the world still under communist rule.

Communist nations in 2004

NEVER FORGOTTEN

American Vietnam war veteran Lou Carello said: *"The war is never going to be over for me. Any man who fought there is going to go to his grave with that war."*
—Quoted in *Vietnam: The Ten Thousand Day War,* Michael Maclear

GENERAL CREIGHTON W. ABRAMS (1914–1974)

Born in Massachusetts in 1914, Abrams had been a U.S. Army officer for 30 years by the time he was appointed deputy commander of MACV in 1967. He took over from General Westmoreland as head of MACV in the summer of 1968 and was in charge during the period of Vietnamization in the war and the withdrawal of U.S. troops. Abrams was appointed U.S. Army Chief of Staff in 1972, a post he held until his death in 1974.

LIEUTENANT WILLIAM L. CALLEY (1944–)

In 1966, at age 23, William Calley dropped out of college and enlisted in the U.S. Army. He was sent to Vietnam in November 1967. Calley was a platoon commander at My Lai hamlet in March 1968, when several hundred Vietnamese civilians were massacred. In 1971, Calley was found guilty of the murder of 22 civilians, although other officers involved in the incident were cleared. Initially given a life sentence, Calley was only briefly imprisoned. Paroled by President Nixon, he was freed and went on to run his father's jewelry store.

WILLIAM COLBY (1920–1996)

Born in Minnesota in 1920, William Colby devoted most of his life to espionage and undercover activity. He was head of the CIA office in Saigon from 1959 to 1962 and returned to Vietnam in 1968 to head the CORDS pacification program and the controversial Operation Phoenix. He was subsequently head of the CIA from 1973 to 1975. Colby died, under somewhat mysterious circumstances, in 1996.

EMPEROR BAO DAI (1913–1997)

Born in Hue in 1913, Bao Dai succeeded his father as emperor of Vietnam—a powerless, ceremonial position—in 1925. He abdicated the throne in 1945, but he was installed as Vietnamese head of state by the French in 1949. After the peace agreement of 1954, Bao Dai was briefly leader of South Vietnam, but the following year he was replaced by his prime minister, Ngo Dinh Diem. Bao Dai died in exile in France in 1997.

PRESIDENT NGO DINH DIEM (1901–1963)

Born in 1901, Diem belonged to Vietnam's Catholic minority. In 1954, he emerged as the United States' preferred choice of leader for South Vietnam and in October 1955 displaced the former emperor, Bao Dai. Diem's rule was marred by corruption and by favoritism toward Catholics, which brought him into conflict with Vietnam's Buddhist majority. In November 1963, he was overthrown in a military coup approved by the United States. Diem was killed in the course of the coup, along with his brother, Ngo Dinh Nhu.

GENERAL VAN TIEN DUNG (1917–2002)

Born in 1917, Dung joined the Indochinese Communist Party in 1937. He played a senior role in the conflicts with France, South Vietnam, and the United States. In 1974, he was appointed commander in chief for the "Ho Chi Minh" campaign, which, the following year, brought about the fall of Saigon. In 1980, he was appointed Vietnam's minister of defense. He died in 2002.

PRESIDENT GERALD FORD (1913–)

Born in Nebraska in 1913, Ford was leader of the Republican minority in Congress before becoming U.S. vice president in 1973 and president in August 1974, upon President Richard Nixon's resignation. Hamstrung by the Democratic majority in Congress, in 1975 he was unable to provide extra aid to the South Vietnamese government, let alone authorize a resumption of U.S. military intervention. Ford was defeated in the 1976 presidential election by Jimmy Carter.

GENERAL VO NGUYEN GIAP (1912–)

Giap was born in Quang Binh province in 1912. After joining the Vietnamese Communist Party, he was arrested by the French colonial authorities in 1930 but soon released. In 1939 Giap was ordered by the party to flee to China to avoid arrest. He joined Ho Chi Minh there. His sister-in-law was executed by the French, however, and his wife and child both died in a French prison. From 1942 to 1945, Giap took part in guerrilla warfare against the Japanese in Vietnam, and from 1946 to 1954 he masterminded the Viet Minh campaign against the French, including the victory at Dien Bien Phu. As defense minister in North Vietnam, he directed the guerrilla war against the South Vietnamese government and U.S. forces up to 1972. His decision to resort to conventional warfare in the 1972 Easter offensive, however, led to heavy losses. Although officially still in his post, he was sidelined during the final takeover of South Vietnam in 1975.

HO CHI MINH (1892–1969)

Born Nguyen That Thanh in 1892 (although on occasion he also claimed a birth date of 1890), Ho left Vietnam for Europe in 1911 and there, in 1920, became a founding member of the French Communist Party. In 1925 Ho moved to China, where he became the leader of Vietnamese exiles dedicated to freeing their country from French rule. He went back to Vietnam in 1941, founding the Viet Minh guerrilla movement. In 1945, he declared Vietnam independent, with himself as president. He led the Viet Minh in the subsequent guerrilla war against France and became president of North Vietnam when the French departed in 1954. He remained the country's leader until his death in 1969.

PRESIDENT LYNDON B. JOHNSON (1908–1973)

Born in Texas in 1908, "LBJ" was a U.S. Senator and a leading figure in the Democratic Party before becoming U.S. vice president under John F. Kennedy in 1961. He assumed the presidency when Kennedy was assassinated in November 1963 and was elected to office in presidential elections the following year. Johnson wanted to be a social reformer, transforming the United States into a fairer "Great Society." But the Vietnam War diverted money and energy from his reform program and subjected Johnson to increasingly harsh criticism. In March 1968, Johnson announced that he would not stand for re-election. He died in 1973.

PRESIDENT JOHN F. KENNEDY (1917–1963)

Born into a wealthy Catholic family in 1917, Kennedy was decorated for bravery in World War II and subsequently entered politics as a Democrat. In 1960, he narrowly defeated Republican Richard Nixon in presidential elections, becoming the youngest elected U.S. president. He was responsible for building up the number of U.S. military advisers in South Vietnam and approved the overthrow of Diem in November 1963. Kennedy was assassinated three weeks after Diem was overthrown. Some people have suggested that Kennedy was on the brink of pulling the United States out of military involvement in Vietnam when he died, but there is no solid evidence for this claim.

HENRY KISSINGER (1923–)

Born in Germany in 1923, Henry Kissinger settled in the United States in 1938. He was a leading academic when, in 1969, he was selected by President Nixon to be his adviser on national security. He dominated U.S. foreign policy under Nixon and became U.S. secretary of state in 1973, a post he continued to hold under President Ford. Kissinger was awarded the Nobel peace prize, jointly with Le Duc Tho, for his part in negotiating the January 1973 Vietnam peace accord.

ROBERT S. MCNAMARA (1916–)

Born in 1916 in San Francisco, McNamara was president of the Ford Motor Company when, in 1961, he was invited to become secretary of defense in the Kennedy administration. In this post, which he also held under President Lyndon Johnson, McNamara was one of the main architects of the Vietnam War. By 1967, however, he had come to believe that the war was a disastrous mistake. He resigned in March 1968 and went on to become president of the World Bank, a position he held until 1981.

GENERAL DUONG VAN MINH (1916–2001)

Known as "Big Minh," South Vietnamese General Doung Van Minh was one of the leaders of the coup that overthrew President Diem in 1963. After the coup, Minh was South Vietnamese head of government for three months before he was himself thrown out of power in a coup. In subsequent years, Minh was a leading opponent of South Vietnam's President Thieu and an advocate for compromise with the communists. Just before the NVA took Saigon in April 1975, Minh became South Vietnamese president, and it was he who formally surrendered the country to the North Vietnamese.

PRESIDENT RICHARD M. NIXON (1913–1994)

Born in California in 1913, Nixon became U.S. vice president in 1952 but lost the 1960 presidential election to the Democrat John F. Kennedy. In a remarkable comeback, Nixon was again chosen as the Republican presidential

candidate in 1968 and won. Nixon was a tough anticommunist and made forceful use of airpower in Southeast Asia, but he fulfilled a promise to get U.S. troops out of Vietnam. His diplomatic initiatives also created a new relationship between the United States and the communist nations China and the Soviet Union. After his re-election in 1972, however, he became involved in the Watergate scandal and was forced to resign the presidency in 1974 to avoid impeachment.

GENERAL LON NOL (1913–1985)

Born in 1913, Cambodian general Lon Nol was a leading figure in his country's government after independence from France in 1955. Under Prince Sihanouk, he served as defense minister, army chief of staff and, later, prime minister. In 1970, Lon Nol overthrew Sihanouk in a coup and seized power, but his efforts to crack down on the Khmer Rouge guerrillas were disastrous. He fled Cambodia in 1975, just before the Khmer Rouge declared victory and took power in the country. Lon Nol died in 1985.

DEAN RUSK (1909–1994)

Born in Georgia in 1909, Rusk held government posts under U.S. president Harry Truman after World War II. Rusk was appointed U.S. secretary of state by President Kennedy in 1961 and continued in the same post under President Johnson. He was a crucial decision-maker during the period when the United States was drawn in to full-scale military involvement in Vietnam. Rusk remained secretary of state until President Nixon took office in 1969. He subsequently became a law professor at the University of Georgia.

NORODOM SIHANOUK (1922–)

Born in 1922, Sihanouk became king of Cambodia in 1941. When Cambodia gained independence from France in 1955, he abdicated the throne but continued to lead, first as prime minister and then as head of state. In 1970, he was overthrown in a coup and formed a government-in-exile in China. He became an unlikely ally of the communist Khmer Rouge, who made him official head of state in 1975. After another period in exile that began in 1979, Sihanouk returned to Cambodia in 1991—once again as head of state, but this time opposing the Khmer Rouge. In 1993, he became king again.

PRESIDENT NGUYEN VAN THIEU (1923–2001)

Born in 1923, Thieu joined the Viet Minh after World War II but soon left because of his opposition to its communist leadership. He then fought for the French in the South Vietnamese Army, which, after 1954, became the ARVN. He was one of the leaders of the 1963 coup against President Diem and took part in military governments over the next four years. In 1967, he was elected president as head of a civilian

government. Reelected unopposed in 1971, he only reluctantly agreed to the 1973 peace accords. In 1975 he fled South Vietnam shortly before the fall of Saigon. Thieu died in 2001.

LE DUC THO (1911–1990)

Born in 1911, Le Duc Tho was a founding member of the Indochinese Communist Party in 1930. He played a leading role in the Viet Minh guerrilla campaign against the French and in organizing the guerrilla war in South Vietnam in the 1960s. He acted as a special adviser to the North Vietnamese delegation at the 1973 Paris peace talks but declined to accept the Nobel peace prize that he was awarded jointly with Henry Kissinger in 1973. He remained a member of Vietnam's leadership until 1986.

GENERAL WILLIAM C. WESTMORELAND (1914–)

William Westmoreland was born in South Carolina in 1914. By the age of 42 he was a major-general in the U.S. Army. In 1964, he was appointed to command the U.S. forces in Vietnam. Westmoreland followed an aggressive strategy, using large formations of troops to seek out and destroy the enemy. U.S. political leaders, however, became increasingly skeptical of his claims to be winning the war, and the Tet offensive fatally undermined his credibility. In the summer of 1968, Westmoreland was brought back to the United States, where he held the post of army chief of staff until his retirement in 1972.

STATISTICS FOR COMBATANT NATIONS

The figures given below for numbers of armed forces indicate (where figures are available) a country's maximum number of personnel operating in Vietnam at any one time and then the total number of people from that country who served in Vietnam from the beginning to the end of the war. Also listed are known casualty figures for both troops and civilians (again, where figures are available).

AUSTRALIA

Personnel in South Vietnam (max.)	approx. 8,000
Total Australians who served in South Vietnam (1965–1971)	59,520

Casualties

Combat deaths	394
Total deaths	501
Wounded	2,069

REPUBLIC OF KOREA (SOUTH KOREA)

Troops in Vietnam (max.)	47,872
Combat deaths	4,407

NEW ZEALAND

Personnel in South Vietnam (max.)	517
Combat deaths	39

THAILAND

Troops in Vietnam (max.)	approx. 10,000
Combat deaths	351

UNITED STATES

Personnel (max., April 30, 1969)	543,482
Total U.S. military personnel served in South Vietnam (1964–1973)	2,594,000

U.S. Casualties

Combat deaths	47,539
Deaths from other causes	10,797
Total dead	58,336*
Wounded	303,704
Severely disabled	75,000

*61 percent of U.S. personnel killed in Vietnam were 21 years of age or younger.

U.S. AIR WAR

Total bombs dropped on Southeast Asia	6.7 million tons

(As a comparison, the total amount of bombs dropped on Germany in World War II was 2.7 million tons)

DEMOCRATIC REPUBLIC OF VIETNAM (NORTH VIETNAM)

Armed forces numbers (1972)

Army	480,000
Air Force	9,000
Navy	3,000
Total combat deaths (including Viet Cong)	440,000
North Vietnamese civilian death (est.)	65,000

REPUBLIC OF VIETNAM (SOUTH VIETNAM)

Armed forces numbers (1971)

Regular forces

Army	410,000
Air Force	50,000
Navy	42,000
Marines	14,000
Total regular	516,000

Territorial forces

Regional forces	284,000
Popular forces	248,000
Total territorial	532,000
Grand total	1,048,000

Casualties for South Vietnam

Military deaths (to 1974)	220,357
Military wounded	499,000
Civilian deaths (estimate)	522,000

1858
France begins conquest of Vietnam.

1930
The Indochinese Communist Party (ICP) is founded by Ho Chi Minh and others.

1941
The Viet Minh movement is founded to fight for Vietnamese independence.

SEPTEMBER 1945
Ho Chi Minh declares Vietnam independent, with himself as president.

NOVEMBER 1946
French forces drive the Viet Minh out of Hanoi and Haiphong.

1949
Communists under Mao Zedong take power in China.

1950–1953
Armed by China, the Viet Minh fight against the French.

MARCH–MAY 1954
The French are defeated by the Viet Minh at Dien Bien Phu.

JULY 1954
Geneva peace accords end the First Indochina War. Ho Chi Minh and his colleagues take power in North Vietnam.

OCTOBER 1955
In South Vietnam, Ngo Dinh Diem defeats former emperor Bao Dai in a referendum and declares himself president of the Republic of Vietnam.

1959
In South Vietnam, guerrilla attacks backed by North Vietnam begin.

1960
Communists found the National Liberation Front (NLF) to coordinate the guerrilla struggle.

1961
President John F. Kennedy sends first U.S. Army helicopter pilots to South Vietnam.

1962
U.S Special Forces (Green Berets) are deployed in South Vietnam.

MAY 1963
Clashes erupt between Vietnamese Buddhists and the Diem regime.

NOVEMBER 2, 1963
Diem is killed during military coup.

NOVEMBER 22, 1963
President Kennedy is assassinated in Dallas, Texas. Lyndon B. Johnson becomes U.S. president.

MAY 1964
General William C. Westmoreland is appointed commander of U.S. forces in Vietnam.

AUGUST 1964
Reports of attacks by the North Vietnamese on U.S. warships in the Gulf of Tonkin lead to a resolution by the U.S. Congress authorizing military action in Vietnam.

FEBRUARY 1965
United States launches air strikes on North Vietnam in retaliation for guerrilla attacks on U.S. bases in South Vietnam.

MARCH 1965
First U.S. Marines land in South Vietnam, officially to defend U.S. bases. "Rolling Thunder," a U.S. bombing campaign against North Vietnam, begins.

NOVEMBER 1965
Battle of Ia Drang Valley, first major encounter between the U.S. Army and the NVA.

1966
U.S. troop levels in Vietnam rise to 385,000. U.S. death toll for the year tops 5,000.

JANUARY 1967
Operation Cedar Falls attacks the guerrilla-dominated Iron Triangle.

FEBRUARY–MAY 1967
Operation Junction City targets communist bases near the Cambodian border.

MAY 1967
Civil Operations and Rural Development Support (CORDS) is established, an organization dedicated to the "pacification" of rural South Vietnam.

SEPTEMBER 1967
Nguyen Van Thieu wins presidential election in South Vietnam.

OCTOBER 1967
Thousands of U.S. antiwar protesters gather around the Pentagon in Washington, D.C., to condemn the war.

JANUARY–APRIL 1968
Siege of the U.S. Marine base at Khe Sanh.

JANUARY–FEBRUARY 1968
Viet Cong and NVA attack South Vietnamese towns and cities in the Tet offensive.

MARCH 1968
Robert McNamara resigns as U.S. defense secretary. President Johnson announces that he will not stand for re-election as president.

JULY 1968
General Abrams replaces General Westmoreland as commander of U.S. forces in Vietnam. The Phoenix program is started, targeting communist activists in South Vietnam.

AUGUST 1968
Antiwar protesters battle with police in Chicago during the Democratic presidential convention.

OCTOBER 1968
Bombing of North Vietnam is halted.

NOVEMBER 1968
Richard Nixon wins United States presidential election.

JANUARY 1969
Peace talks begin in Paris.

MARCH 1969
Nixon authorizes the secret bombing of Cambodia.

APRIL 1969
U.S. troop levels in Vietnam peak at 543,482.

MAY 1969
Battle of Hamburger Hill in the A Shau Valley.

JUNE 1969
Nixon announces the first U.S. troop withdrawals and that priority is to be given to "Vietnamization."

SEPTEMBER 1969
The president of North Vietnam, Ho Chi Minh, dies.

MARCH 1970
In Cambodia, General Lon Nol takes power in a coup that deposes Norodom Sihanouk.

APRIL–JUNE 1970
U.S. and ARVN forces carry out an incursion into Cambodia.

MAY 4, 1970
Four young antiwar demonstrators are shot dead by U.S. National Guard members at Kent State University, Ohio.

JUNE 1970
U.S. Congress repeals the Gulf of Tonkin Resolution.

JANUARY–APRIL 1971
ARVN forces carry out incursion into Laos.

FEBRUARY 1971
President Nixon visits China and holds talks with Chinese leader Mao Zedong.

MARCH 1971
U.S. Army lieutenant William Calley is found guilty of the killings of Vietnamese civilians at My Lai hamlet in March 1968.

AUGUST 1971
Australia and New Zealand announce withdrawal of troops from Vietnam.

MARCH 30, 1972
North Vietnam opens its Easter Offensive against South Vietnam.

APRIL–OCTOBER 1972
U.S. "Linebacker 1" air bombing campaign against North Vietnam.

APRIL–JULY 1972
NVA siege of An Loc resisted by ARVN forces with support of U.S. airpower.

MAY 1, 1972
Quang Tri City falls to the NVA.

SEPTEMBER 16, 1972
Quang Tri City recaptured by ARVN forces.

OCTOBER 1972
Breakthrough announced in Paris peace talks.

DECEMBER 18–30, 1972
B-52 bombers batter North Vietnamese cities in "Operation Linebacker 2."

JANUARY 27, 1973
Peace agreement signed in Paris.

MARCH 29, 1973
Last U.S. troops leave Vietnam.

AUGUST 1973
U.S. Congress forces a halt to the bombing of Cambodia.

AUGUST 1974
President Nixon resigns after the Watergate scandal. Gerald Ford becomes U.S. president.

SEPTEMBER 1974
President Ford announces a partial amnesty for Vietnam War deserters and draft evaders.

JANUARY 1975
The NVA seizes a South Vietnamese provincial capital, Phuoc Binh. The North Vietnamese leadership approves a plan for the final defeat of South Vietnam.

MARCH 1975
The ARVN crumbles in the face of an NVA offensive. The northern half of South Vietnam is abandoned to NVA forces.

APRIL 17, 1975
The Cambodian capital of Phnom Penh falls to the Khmer Rouge.

21 APRIL 1975
South Vietnamese president Thieu resigns as NVA forces approach the capital city of Saigon.

APRIL 30, 1975
NVA forces enter Saigon as the last U.S. personnel flee. South Vietnam surrenders.

DECEMBER 1975
Laos becomes the communist People's Democratic Republic.

1976
The Socialist Republic of Vietnam is founded, combining North and South Vietnam. Saigon is renamed Ho Chi Minh City.

JANUARY 1977
U.S. president Jimmy Carter pardons most Vietnam War draft evaders.

DECEMBER 1978
Vietnam invades Cambodia (Kampuchea), ousting the Khmer Rouge regime the following month.

FEBRUARY–MARCH 1979
Border war erupts between China and Vietnam.

1989
Vietnamese forces withdraw from Cambodia.

1995
Relations between Vietnam and the United States are normalized.

GLOSSARY

17th parallel A line of latitude 17 degrees north of the equator, chosen as the dividing line between North and South Vietnam.

air cavalry U.S. troop formations using fleets of helicopters to advance to the battlefield.

airlift Delivery of supplies or troops by air.

Army of the Republic of Vietnam (ARVN) The army of South Vietnam.

artillery Large guns or other heavy arms.

atrocity Massacre or other act of extreme brutality, especially by soldiers against civilians in a time of war.

besieged Encircled and under heavy attack by an enemy.

Buddhist A person who follows Buddhism, a religion founded in India in the fifth century B.C. by Siddhartha Gautama ("Buddha"). It is popular throughout Asia.

Central Intelligence Agency (CIA) A U.S. agency, established in 1947, that gathers intelligence and conducts covert operations in foreign countries.

Civil Operations and Rural Development Support (CORDS) An organization established in South Vietnam to encourage loyalty to the South Vietnamese government among people in rural areas.

Civilian Irregular Defense Groups (CIDGs) Guerrilla forces organized by U.S. Special Forces in remote areas of South Vietnam.

coalition A partnership of different political parties that share power in a country's government.

colony A territory or country that is ruled by another country, often to exploit its resources.

communism: a system of government in which the government owns all or most property and controls the economy. It usually involves one-party, authoritarian rule.

Cold War Rivalry between the United States and the Soviet Union, as well as their respective allies, that lasted from 1945 to 1991.

concentration camp A place where people such as prisoners of war, political prisoners, or persecuted minorities are held, often under harsh conditions.

conventional warfare Conflicts that involve regular armed forces engaged in open, direct combat, usually with heavy arms and equipment.

counterinsurgency Actions or programs to suppress an insurgency, or guerrilla movement.

coup The overthrow of a country's government, often by officers of that country's armed forces.

covert Carried out in secret.

defoliants Chemicals that kill trees and other plants by destroying their leaves.

democratic Term used for a government that is freely elected by a country's citizens.

demilitarized zone (DMZ) A stretch of land that separated North and South Vietnam, where military forces could not operate.

domino theory During the Cold War, the belief that if one country in a region fell under communist control, then neighboring countries would each fall in turn, like a row of dominoes.

draft The selection of people for compulsory, or involuntary, military service.

ethnic Having to do with a group of people of the same race, culture, religion, or place of origin.

firebase In Vietnam, a base where heavy artillery was stationed to provide support for infantry patrolling the surrounding countryside.

garrison A place where troops are stationed.

guerrilla Having to do with a kind of warfare involving small, mobile groups of soldiers who are not part of a regular army and who often use hit-and-run ambush attacks to fight against more heavily armed conventional forces.

gunships Fixed-wing aircraft or helicopters armed with a powerful array of guns and missiles, used to attack troops on the ground.

imperialist Having to do with a country's expansion of its empire through occupation or control of other territories or countries.

incursion A hostile penetration, by armed forces, into a region or country.

infantry An army's foot soldiers.

intelligence In a military context, information about an enemy's movements or plans.

Khmer Rouge A communist guerrilla group in Cambodia that ruled the country, which it renamed Kampuchea, from 1975 to 1979.

logistical support The equipment and supplies, such as ammunition, fuel, and food, needed to keep armed forces in operation.

Military Assistance Command, Vietnam (MACV) During the Vietnam War, the central headquarters of the U.S. military in South Vietnam.

military personnel Any people working in the armed forces of a country.

militia A group of civilians who are armed to defend their particular area.

napalm A gasoline-based substance that bursts into flames upon contact with air and was dropped by U.S. aircraft during the Vietnam War.

National Liberation Front (NLF) The official name for the guerrilla movement in South Vietnam.

nationalist In the context of the Vietnam conflict, a person who wanted Vietnam to become an independent, unified nation.

North Vietnamese Army (NVA) The armed forces of North Vietnam, which, along with Viet Cong guerrillas, fought against ARVN and US. forces.

pacification During the Vietnam War, the practice of establishing secure government control over areas of South Vietnam where communist guerrillas had been active.

power vacuum A situation in which there are no leaders with clear control.

regime A system of government, or a group of people who rule a country.

resolution A formal proposal agreed by a vote.

self-sustaining Able to continue without outside support.

Soviet Union A communist nation that was made up of Russia and neighboring republics and existed from 1922 to 1991.

subversion The undermining of a country's government through actions within that country.

Viet Cong Name used for communist guerrillas who operated in South Vietnam.

Vietnamization The U.S. military's effort to make ARVN forces take the primary role in fighting against communist forces.

RECOMMENDED BOOKS

The following books about the Vietnam War are recommended for young readers:

De Capua, Sarah E. *The Vietnam Memorial* (*Cornerstones of Freedom* series). Children's Press, 2003.

Dowswell, Paul. *The Vietnam War* (*The Cold War* series). World Almanac Library, 2002.

Gavin, Philip. *The Fall of Vietnam* (*World History* series). Lucent Books, 2003.

Myers, Walter Dean. *Patrol: An American Soldier in Vietnam.* HarperCollins, 2002.

Steele, Philip. *Ho Chi Minh* (*Leading Lives* series). Heinemann Library, 2003.

Willoughby, Douglas. *The Vietnam War* (*20th Century Perspectives* series). Heinemann Library, 2001.

The following books provide more detailed accounts of the Vietnam War. In these books, use the Table of Contents or Index to learn more about a particular battle or aspect of the war:

Corbett, Robin. *Guerrilla Warfare.* Trans-Atlantic Publications, 1987.

Currey, Cecil B. *Victory at Any Cost: the Genius of Viet Nam's Gen. Vo Nguyen Giap.* Brasseys, Inc., 2000.

Fall, Bernard B. *Street Without Joy.* Stackpole Books, 1994.

Lewy, Guenter. *America in Vietnam.* Oxford University Press, 1980.

Maclear, Michael. *Vietnam: The Ten Thousand Day War.* Methuen, 1981.

Mann, Robert. *A Grand Delusion: America's Descent into Vietnam.* Basic Books, 2002.

Scholl-Latour, Peter. *Death in the Rice Fields: An Eyewitness Account of Vietnam's Three Wars 1945–1979.* Penguin USA, 1986.

Sheehan, Neil. *A Bright Shining Lie: John Paul Vann and America in Vietnam.* Random House, 1988.

Summers, Harry G. Jr. *Historical Atlas of the Vietnam War.* Houghton Mifflin, 1995.

The following books provide firsthand accounts of the combat experience in Vietnam:

Broyles, William Jr. *Brothers in Arms: A Journey from War to Peace.* Avon, 1987.

Caputo, Philip. *A Rumor of War.* Owl Books, 1996.

Donovan, David. *Once a Warrior King: Memories of an Officer in Vietnam.* Ballantine Books, 1986.

Mason, Robert. *Chickenhawk.* Viking Press, 1984.

Moore, Lt. Gen. Harold G. and Joseph L. Galloway. *We Were Soldiers Once . . . and Young.* Perennial, 1993.

O'Brien, Tim. *If I Die in a Combat Zone.* Dell Publishing, 1989.

RECOMMENDED VIDEOS

The following documentaries about the Vietnam War are available on VHS or DVD:

The Anderson Platoon (1990), Home Vision Entertainment

Archives of War: Volume Six, Vietnam (2000), MPI Home Video

National Geographic: Vietnam's Unseen War (2002), Warner Home Video

Vietnam: A Television History (1997), WGBH Boston Video

Vietnam: In the Year of the Pig (1999), MPI Home Video

The Vietnam War with Walter Cronkite (2003), Edi Video

Vietnam: Ten Thousand Day War (1998), Ghadar and Associates

The War at Home (1998), First Run Feature

RECOMMENDED WEB SITES

http://web.uccs.edu/~history/index/vietnam.html
A guide to resources and research sources on the Vietnam war that are available on the Internet.
www.lcweb.loc.gov/folklife/vets
An official oral history web site that includes firsthand accounts of the Vietnam War.
www.pbs.org/wgbh/amex/vietnam
Part of the WGBH *American Experience* series, "Vietnam Online" includes an interactive time line and other features.
www.spartacus.schoolnet.co.uk/vietnam.html
Covers personalities, events, and issues of the war and also provides links to related web sites.
www.WomenInVietnam.com
Provides fascinating material about the often-overlooked role of women in the Vietnam War.

Note to parents and teachers

Every effort has been made by the publishers to ensure that these web sites are suitable for children; that they are of the highest educational value; and that they contain no inappropriate or offensive material. The nature of the Internet, however, makes it impossible to guarantee that the contents of these sites will not be altered. We strongly advise that a responsible adult supervise Internet access.

PLACES TO VISIT

Popularly known as "The Wall," The Vietnam Veterans Memorial, in Washington, D.C., is a national memorial that includes a black granite structure engraved with the names of more than 58,000 members of the U.S. armed forces who were killed or declared missing in action during the Vietnam War. For information:

Vietnam Veterans Memorial
900 Ohio Drive, SW
Washington, D.C. 20024
Tel: 202-426-6841
Web site: *www.nps.gov/vive/*

The New Jersey Vietnam Veteran's Memorial and the Vietnam Era Educational Center
1 Memorial Lane
PNC Bank Arts Center
Garden State Parkway, Exit 116
Holmdel, NJ 07733
Tel: 732-335-0033
Web site: *www.njvvmf.org/*

National Vietnam Veterans Art Museum
1801 South Indiana Avenue
Chicago, IL 60616
Tel: 312-326-0270

Gallery Vietnam
345 Greenwich Street
New York, NY 10013
Tel: 212-431-8889
Web site: *www.galleryvietnam.com*

ABOUT THE AUTHOR

The author, Reg Grant, studied history at the University of Oxford and is the author of more than a dozen books on modern history. He specializes in the history of the twentieth century. His book *The Holocaust* (1997) was short-listed for the *Times Educational Supplement*'s Senior Information Book Award.